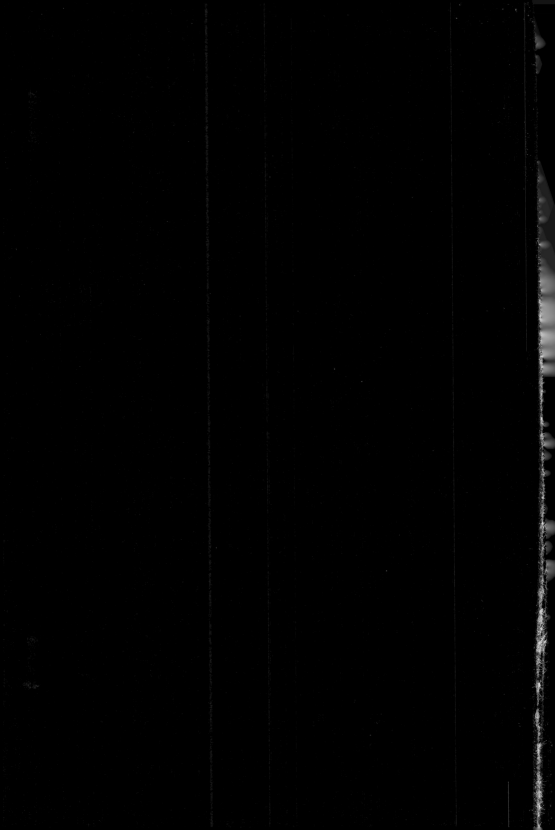

UNACCOUNTABLE
TRUTH AND LIES
ON
PARLIAMENT HILL

UNACCOUNTABLE

TRUTH AND LIES ON PARLIAMENT HILL

KEVIN PAGE

with
Vern Stenlund

VIKING

VIKING
an imprint of Penguin Canada Books Inc., a Penguin Random House Company

Published by the Penguin Group
Penguin Canada Books Inc., 320 Front Street West, Suite 1400, Toronto, Ontario M5V 3B6, Canada

Penguin Group (USA) LLC, 375 Hudson Street, New York, New York 10014, U.S.A.
Penguin Books Ltd, 80 Strand, London WC2R 0RL, England
Penguin Ireland, 25 St Stephen's Green, Dublin 2, Ireland (a division of Penguin Books Ltd)
Penguin Group (Australia), 707 Collins Street, Melbourne, Victoria 3008, Australia
(a division of Pearson Australia Group Pty Ltd)
Penguin Books India Pvt Ltd, 11 Community Centre, Panchsheel Park, New Delhi – 110 017, India
Penguin Group (NZ), 67 Apollo Drive, Rosedale, Auckland 0632, New Zealand
(a division of Pearson New Zealand Ltd)
Penguin Books (South Africa) (Pty) Ltd, 24 Sturdee Avenue, Rosebank, Johannesburg 2196, South Africa

Penguin Books Ltd, Registered Offices: 80 Strand, London WC2R 0RL, England

First published 2015

3 4 5 6 7 8 9 10 (RRD)

Copyright © Kevin Page, 2015

Manufactured in the U.S.A.

LIBRARY AND ARCHIVES CANADA CATALOGUING IN PUBLICATION

Page, Kevin, 1957-, author
Unaccountable / Kevin Page.
Includes bibliographical references and index.
ISBN 978-0-670-06816-6 (bound)

1. Government accountability—Canada. 2. Canada. Office
of the Parliamentary Budget Officer. 3. Political planning—Canada.
4. Canada—Politics and government—21st century.

I. Title.

JL75.P23 2015   352.3'50971   C2015-901096-9

eBook ISBN 9780143194378

Visit the Penguin Canada website at **www.penguin.ca**

Special and corporate bulk purchase rates available; please see
www.penguin.ca/corporatesales or call 1-800-810-3104.

I dedicate this book to my wife, Julia. Her love and personal courage during the most difficult times that any parent could ever have to endure were, and still remain, an inspiration to me. I love you.

I dedicate this book to my children, Jesse and Chelsey, two wonderful people who make their parents so very proud.

I dedicate this book to every member of my family, as well as to my extended family of friends. In these relationships I continue to find great strength and purpose.

And lastly, and very specifically, I dedicate this book to my late son, Tyler. I owe him for giving me the courage to try. In the struggle, I found new meaning.

CONTENTS

PROLOGUE

It was early on the afternoon of May 3, 2012, when I walked into a meeting room on Parliament Hill to confer with members of the Standing Committee on Public Accounts. My attendance at that meeting had been requested given my role at the time as Canada's first ever parliamentary budget officer (PBO). The PBO was a position that had been conceived, created, and embedded in the law of the land by the Conservative Party of Canada, the governing party in Ottawa. It was intended to be an independent office with the primary duty of scrutinizing proposed government spending to protect the interests of all Canadians. I had been appointed to the position by Prime Minister Stephen Harper himself, and my five-year term was fast coming to an end. A career public servant, I had accepted the position knowing full well that it would probably be my last stop within the ranks of the civil service.

This particular meeting was hardly business as usual. The main topic for discussion was the government's proposed purchase of the F-35 fighter plane, a procurement that would be the largest military purchase of capital equipment in recent memory. But this meeting was not only about buying planes. More importantly, this was about trust, accountability, and fiscal management on the part of our federal government. Why? Because Auditor General Michael Ferguson had called the government to task on the purchase. He had rattled its chains with his own findings about the F-35s, effectively demonstrating that civil servants had gone to cabinet with projected numbers that were even larger than those we had forecasted at the PBO a year earlier. Yet all the while, the public reports emanating from the government estimated smaller numbers. At the same time, politicians were criticizing the PBO analysis as incorrect. Something didn't add up. Once the auditor general's report went public, the need for this meeting had become apparent. It represented an opportunity to put the F-35 procurement back on the rails.

When Terry Milewski, a senior correspondent from the CBC, walks in to such a meeting, you know that there's going to be national coverage, and there he was. By the time I entered the building, there were already other members of the press gathering in the hallway outside the meeting room. This was going to be an interesting mix of politicians, civil servants, and media. As I made my way into the room, I observed many of the heavy hitters in town in attendance, all lined up according to party affiliation with loyalties clearly stitched onto their sleeves. The government had decided to purchase the F-35s and the forecasts of those costs were in dispute. Members of the Conservative government involved in this purchase had appeared very self-assured in the days leading up to the announcement of their plans. The F-35s carried a hefty price tag—and those costs would be borne by the taxpayers of Canada. But I had my doubts about the government's projections. My team at the Parliamentary Budget Office believed that due diligence was lacking, and I was prepared to state that for the record. The government had estimated that the total bill for such a piece of military hardware would be somewhere between $9 billion and $16 billion, dependent upon the costing framework and the anticipated useful life cycle of such a plane. Our research showed that their budgeted numbers were far below the actual likely full costs for such a purchase. And so, what might have been just another day in Ottawa, just another meeting with bureaucrats, just another day on the job as the parliamentary budget officer, became much more.

This had turned into a highly charged event. The chair of the committee, David Christopherson, went out of his way to lay ground rules so as to create a forum for meaningful discussion. At the beginning of the meeting, I took a quick visual scan of the room as our presentation was being distributed. The Conservative backbenchers did not appear to be a happy bunch. I knew we had the right numbers, and I could see that reality reflected back at me through their expressions. I looked over to my left and noticed that Bob Rae was in the room. I remember thinking how unusual that was because he wasn't a member of this committee, and his presence signalled to me that the stakes were high. Rae was in attendance to observe and gather information in preparation for his next discussions of the F-35s with people from the Department of National Defence (DND).

I wasn't sure how Conservative members were going to behave, given the auditor general's determinations. I should have known. They knew the numbers yet there they were—lined up shoulder to shoulder, like so many Roman centurions with shields up and ready to serve their Caesar. They weren't in that room because of their gift for independent thought. Rather, they were in attendance because of a call for loyalty.

We were subjected to a full range of questions and insinuations that day by committee members, from technical inquiries designed to raise uncertainty about our numbers to nonsensical questions that were clearly an attempt to intimidate. We had hoped for a meeting of substance; what we received instead was

stonewalling and rhetoric. As I first watched and then partici-
pated in the proceedings, I felt anger building within me, inspired
by all of the political yes-men and -women who appeared willing
to vote blindly on issues that could potentially affect Canadians
from coast to coast. There wasn't a lot of guts in that group of
sentries, I thought.

As I left the meeting and made my way down the hall, I
suddenly found myself engulfed in a sea of reporters and cameras.
I was funnelled toward a particular spot in the Hall of Honour,
where a media scrum was set to take place. Many of the press
corps had been at the meeting and heard the discussions. They
had followed me out the door when the proceedings had
concluded, expecting some commentary on what had just trans-
pired from the perspective of the Parliamentary Budget Office.
Yes, the press can smell a story all right. The cameras began to
flash and video started to roll as things got underway. That's quite
a place to be, front and centre and in full view of all those lenses.
Microphones and audio recorders are stuck in your face. Questions
are shouted at you, one on top of another and in rapid succession.
There isn't much physical space in which to manoeuvre during
one of those scrums. People crowd in around you from all directions to better hear your responses. It's almost claustrophobic.

After a few minutes of back and forth with the media, I
noticed a PBO colleague slowly making his way toward me—
Mostafa Askari was coming to get me the hell out of there. Seeing
Mostafa told me that it was almost time for the camera lights to
go dark. But then, in an instant, things turned—as if someone
had decided, "Not so fast, buddy, you're not off the hook yet."

It started with the query about the existence of two sets of
books on the F-35 proposed purchase, a contentious issue all by
itself. I got through that sequence in a routine kind of way. But
then *the* question was delivered, concise and pointed. Perhaps

the reporter who delivered the question, Julie Van Dusen, had a sense about my mood at the time. Maybe my body language gave away my personal angst at that moment, though I'm told that my face doesn't show much emotion. Perhaps it was simply the time and place—the right question by the right person at the right moment. Van Dusen asked, "To be clear, are you suggesting that the government really wanted Canadians to think these planes [the F-35s] would cost a lot less money?"

I started to answer about the concept of life cycle costs as they relate to total expenditures for such a purchase. The economist in me was taking over. I could swear I saw her roll her eyes as the words came fumbling out of my mouth. She stopped me in mid-sentence, basically disregarding my answer. She wanted clarity, so again she asked, "Are you suggesting that the government wanted Canadians to think that these planes would cost a lot less money?"

It was a direct question, a touchy question, one with a lot of political implications. Van Dusen was representing all of her press colleagues on this one—all Canadians for that matter—and they deserved a direct answer for a change. But when it's *you* that has been on a professional hot seat for an extended period of time and it's *your* mug that is being splashed across television sets from Vancouver to St. John's, your instinct is to try and get around a direct question with some kind of an indirect answer. You try to temporarily appease the interviewer. That was where I initially tried to take it, but Van Dusen was relentless. I couldn't dodge the question forever. She had zeroed in, and never took her eyes off me. I turned for a moment and briefly looked behind me, the question still ringing in my ears. It must have appeared as if I was checking the darkened portion of the corridor to see if anyone from the government was watching or listening (a nonsensical idea given that we were at that moment live on national television). Then, suddenly, I just didn't really give a damn anymore. As I turned back toward the scrum, I blurted out my answer. "Yes," I said.

There was a moment of stunned silence, followed by some looks of disbelief from the assembled members of the press. That became an instant in my life, and in the life of the office of the PBO, that has stood as a sort of flashpoint for many people in this country who were watching TV that day. It spoke to the potentially important role that the parliamentary budget officer could play in our democratic system of governance. It was a moment in which that one word—"Yes"—set off a controversy that would become headline news. I would go on to finish my five-year term but not before being attacked at every juncture by the very group of politicians that had seen to my appointment. Before I was done as PBO, the minister of finance would declare me "unreliable, unbelievable, and incredible."

William Gladstone, a former chancellor of the Exchequer and a four-time prime minister of the United Kingdom, warned in 1891 that "if the House of Commons by any responsibility loses the power of the control of public money, depend on it, your very liberty will be worth very little in comparison." I fear that this is exactly what is happening in our country. The F-35 debacle is "Exhibit A." Canada's House of Commons has lost the power of the purse and members of Parliament (MPs) spend little time scrutinizing spending. Currently our MPs routinely vote on legislation without knowledge of policy specifics and their related financial implications. Real debate with analysis on Parliament Hill is virtually dead. Successive Liberal and Conservative governments have made this happen while the vast majority of the public service have silently stood by and watched.

Stéphane Hessel, a freedom fighter in the French Resistance during World War II, said in his book *A Time for Outrage* that the worst of all attitudes is indifference. He notes that as individuals we all have a responsibility to make our society better. Sadly, I sense that many Canadians, civil servants included, have settled into a place of indifference. We are disconnected from our Parliament. We have lost trust in our political leaders and public servants. Our collective response, increasingly, is to turn our heads, look the other way, shrug our shoulders, and hope that somehow all will be well. But it won't!

Canadians from all political persuasions need to appreciate that the institutions of government in this country matter. Historically, the prosperity of the citizenry depended on them. That hasn't changed in modern times. They matter because, when properly functioning, those same institutions act to preserve and strengthen our democracy. In their 2012 book, *Why Nations Fail*, economists Daron Acemoglu and James A. Robinson argue that the ability of legislatures to hold governments to account is a key determining factor in the history of any country.

The 2015 federal election represents a critical time for the restoration of trust, debate, and scrutiny within Canada. Most importantly, it represents a critical time to restore the power of the purse to members of the House of Commons where it rightly belongs. That is my motivation for writing this book. We need to end our indifference. We need to reinvigorate our institutions so as to take on the challenges and issues of the twenty-first century. We owe that to our children, our grandchildren, and all generations of Canadians to come.

ONE

SET UP TO FAIL

In 2006, Canadians were being courted by our national political parties as a federal election was about to be fought. Paul Martin was the sitting prime minister but his position was tenuous. The Liberals had been taken to task by their political opponents and the media in what had become a messy political affair centred in Quebec, generally referred to as the "Sponsorship Scandal" or "Sponsorgate." There was a stench of scandal, a kind of corruption associated with the federal government because of the perceived misappropriation of funds in that province for the better part of a decade, beginning in 1996. The Liberals went from the frying pan into the fire when Sheila Fraser, then auditor general, revealed damning findings about the particulars of Sponsorgate. The Gomery Commission of inquiry soon followed and its investigation spelled disaster for Prime Minister Martin and his party. The words *scandal* and *corruption* are never a welcome sound on the campaign trail, and in the case of the Liberal Party, unfortunately (or fortunately, depending on your political affiliations), those words stuck. The Sponsorgate scandal would play a major role in the outcome of the 2006 federal election.

As voting day approached, Stephen Harper, then leader of the official opposition, had made several campaign promises in the

event that the election went his way. One of them was precipi-
tated by what he and his Conservative colleagues perceived as
the lack of openness on the part of the governing Liberals. It was
all about accountability, he claimed, and so Harper announced
that, if elected, he had a plan to create a more fiscally transparent
Parliament Hill. He stated that as prime minister he was prepared
to establish an independent budget authority that would deliver
a form of objective analysis for members of Parliament and
related parliamentary committees. The person appointed to the
position would provide insights about the state of the nation's
finances, including trends in the national economy, as well as the
financial cost of proposals under consideration by either House.
Specifically, it would be an independent budget authority which
would assist the government and members of Parliament on all
manner of things financial, including forecasting economic and
fiscal planning environments; costing new government programs;
and scrutinizing proposed departmental spending authorities.

Harper had assailed the Liberals for concealing information from opposition party members. He was indignant at the
closed ranks and barriers the Liberals had created. It's important
to emphasize that the Parliamentary Budget Office was proposed
by Harper to overcome that lack of transparency and the lack
of accountability. When I first looked at the terms of reference
proposed for the new agency, I quickly came to appreciate that, if
properly implemented, this initiative might have a lasting and
positive effect on the political landscape of the country. It could
operate similarly to the Congressional Budget Office (CBO) in
the United States, an agency long respected and trusted in that
country among politicians, public servants, and the public at large.

The newly minted Prime Minister Harper fulfilled his
campaign promise and in December 2006 passed the
Accountability Act, which was the enabling legislation that

amended the act of Parliament. There would be a parliamentary budget officer. The position carried with it a name and a mandate. Well, it had a name anyway. The mandate part would become another issue altogether over time.

Once the position had been created, it initially appeared that few qualified people wanted to sign up for the assignment. After all, there was a certain kind of "kill the messenger" aspect to the job. If you delivered independently researched, unbiased information to Parliament about costs, you risked facing the wrath of the executive that had appointed you to the position in the first place, especially if your estimates contradicted the government's. Within the existing civil service culture in Canada, there had never been a mechanism that provided for open disagreement with government financial policy. Unlike the American example of the Congressional Budget Office in Washington, Ottawa was a closed shop.

The corollary would be to simply say nice things about the government in power, but then you would face the ridicule and scorn of the media and the Canadian populace for being too soft on the government. It appeared to be a no-win scenario. The perception among many senior-level civil servants was that taking the position would mean the end of their public service career, one way or another. There weren't a lot of people waiting in line to sign up for that kind of assignment.

I also had the feeling that Canadians could not distinguish between the purpose of a PBO and that of the Office of the Auditor General within our parliamentary system. There were questions about why Parliament needed both an auditor general *and* a parliamentary budget officer. Wouldn't they basically do the same thing—track money? There was confusion about the respective mandates and the tools used within both offices.

To clarify, the work of a Parliamentary Budget Office (PBO) is fundamentally different from the work that occurs out of a national audit office (AG). A high functioning PBO should be responsible for financial due diligence before Parliament spends money. That is, it has to look ahead and forecast. The PBO was designed to "kick the tires" on a business case *before* public money is ever spent. That mandate could be a tough sell in an environment where the public service is somewhat secretive. It could be even more daunting when you have a government that often appears to make decisions based more on ideological grounds than on economic and financial analysis and fact. Actual economic data is updated every day. So, as John Maynard Keynes said, "When the facts change, I change my mind." The person in charge at the PBO would have to be prepared to change course as new economic details emerged. The tool box of a budget officer would include many economic and costing models, some of which would have to be developed in-house on a just-in-time basis.

The work of the auditor general, in comparison, is opposite to that of the PBO. The AG carries out financial due diligence *after* the money has been spent. The AG's audit tools focus on such issues as financial control and performance relative to policy and plans. This can be controversial as well. When scandals emerge, such as those involving cost overruns related to the gun registry or Senate expenses, auditors are brought in to clean up the mess. It is high-profile work but it occurs after the proverbial horse has left the barn. There is an old expression among economists that "The auditors come in to bayonet the wounded." It's a tough metaphor, but the implication is obvious.

I believe we have an imbalance between up-front financial analysis and ex post analysis, with too little of the former. Certainly, MPs need both if they are to perform their elected duties to the best of their abilities. The parliamentary budget officer and the auditor general should function like bookends bracketing public spending. However, the power of the purse in the House of Commons depends most importantly on MPs having sound financial information *before* they commit to a vote that will spend taxpayer monies. Then we wouldn't need as much bayoneting of the wounded. Unfortunately, it seems that those in power with a four- to five-year term like to do things with little debate. When they are wrong, they simply ask for forgiveness later.

But I digress. At its core, the parliamentary budget officer position as created in 2006 was to be responsible for forecasting the cost of purchases resulting from specific policies. That can be a very complex undertaking. Perhaps the easiest way to explain this is to compare it to buying an automobile.

Let's say that the car you want to purchase has a sticker price of $30 000. That's fine, but of course, that is just the base price. You must also factor in such things as the tax that will be applied to the initial purchase price of the vehicle, and depending on which jurisdiction that occurs in, those numbers will vary. You will also need licence plates, and those cost money. You need to fill the car with gas, keep the tires in good repair, and so on. Those are maintenance costs that don't show up in the sticker price, but they exist nevertheless. But let's stay on that initial purchase price for just a moment longer. If you want a certain type of automobile within a certain class of car, that thirty grand might only give you a basic model. No leather seats, no trim package, no sun roof, and so on. If you want all the options available on that vehicle, the price might go as high as $40 000. It would be foolish to purchase a product that does not meet your needs, or wants. It might mean that if certain options are deemed absolutely necessary (heated seats?) then you might have to go down a notch in the "prestige" department and find a different car that would provide what you want within the framework of the pricing you know you can afford. You need to be truthful about what you will have to pay or else you will run into financial stress down the road.

Similarly, the duty of the PBO is to provide *sound* forecasting so that everything is transparent and understandable. The job was not to create policy, protect turf, or defend anyone or any department. Simply, the job was *to do the job that economists need to do*: forecast real costs so that the decision makers could make *informed* decisions.

However, in practical terms, given party partisanship and given that all governments spin information for the media, the new PBO position would not be an easy ride. Telling a prime minster or a finance minister that the government's projections are off base could be dangerous to your civil service livelihood. Those people might not like hearing that they cannot afford that car with all the options. As a result, the PBO position remained vacant for a considerable amount of time.

Other factors involving the new Harper government also may have made people hesitate to apply for the PBO position. In 2007, Linda Keen, then the CEO and president of the Canadian Nuclear Safety Commission, was suddenly and summarily dismissed from the commission amid a great deal of acrimony. She had disagreed with the government on an issue within her portfolio that she felt was fundamental to the integrity of her position, and her stance eventually led to her dismissal. The episode took on a particularly negative tone as she exited the job—the government bad mouthed her mercilessly as the door was slammed behind Keen. Anyone who might have been remotely interested in the PBO position must have watched that entire Keen affair in horror and reconsidered. It certainly scared away some qualified candidates and it left a very bad taste in my mouth.

This apparent strategy—labelling anyone who might offer any opposition, combined with launching a kind of scorched-earth personal attack—was a trend that would unfortunately be repeated far too often in the years ahead. The government consistently attempted to discredit people who stood in opposition on the Hill or dared to disagree with its programs or policies. It did a lot of "spinning" in order to secure votes, and personal attacks were not outside the boundaries. It was the Conservative modus operandi and became an undeniable pattern over time.

Another deterrent was the way in which the newly created Parliamentary Budget Office was structured. When the Accountability Act was rolled out, it was revealed that the new officer would be positioned as a mid-level bureaucrat instead of at the senior levels of government. That was a problem, given the hierarchical nature of the civil service. Furthermore, there was the fact that Harper had never seemed to have any affinity for the public service, whether in his role as opposition leader or during his tenure as prime minister. He appeared to believe that the public service was dominated by a group of Liberal loyalist holdovers from the successive Liberal governments that had occupied 24 Sussex Drive since the 1990s. The new prime minister seemed to view the public service as an agency that operated counter to the Conservatives' agenda. Public servants could not be trusted based on their perceived political bias.

And yet another factor likely proved discouraging to possible applicants: the parliamentary budget officer would stay on the job at the leisure of the prime minister and could be fired at his discretion.

There was virtually no role for Parliament in any of this, which was and still is a problem—a very *big* problem. In theory, parliamentarians would be the primary benefactors of this new position, yet they would have no say in its appointment or its function. The PBO was not created as an officer of Parliament but rather as an officer of the Library of Parliament, a significant difference. Making the PBO an officer of Parliament would have meant that the chosen person would then be responsible to Parliament for scrutinizing both the legislative mandate and administration of taxpayer monies. The person would have reported to the speakers of both the House of Commons and the Senate. Instead, the government wanted the parliamentary budget officer to report to the parliamentary librarian. The new reporting structure made little sense: there was very little overlap between the work of the parliamentary librarian and the mandate of the new parliamentary budget officer. Overall, it seemed that what *Opposition Leader* Harper proposed wasn't what *Prime Minister* Harper delivered.

The 2006 Conservative Party platform, "Stand up for Canada," focused on a handful of policy priorities. "Stand up for Accountability" was priority number one, and in it creating a parliamentary budget officer featured prominently. The platform language highlighted the creation of an "independent" authority and the requirement for government departments to provide timely information. Both got watered down in letter and in spirit, in law and in practice. For practitioners, an independent authority would imply provisions in appointment, tenure, and structure of office that would resemble officers such as the auditor general. This would include protections for independence like appointment procedures that involved competence and approval by Parliament, not just by the prime minister. It should include provisions for dismissal that went beyond the "pleasure" of the prime minister. The accountability wine got seriously watered down as Harper made the transition from opposition leader to prime minister.

The disconnect extended even to the physical location of the PBO offices. Initially, those offices were scattered across different parts of the Library of Parliament, making it a clumsy operation on all fronts, disruptive and designed (in my opinion, of course) to make life as complicated as possible for the PBO team. This appears to have been yet another attempt to get the PBO into a lapdog position for the first five years of its existence. The problem with that scenario was that the group of people who would eventually comprise the PBO never viewed themselves as lapdogs. And, as time would reveal, when push came to shove that particular group of dogs had some bite in them.

There were other speed bumps early on. One civil servant who eventually took a position at the PBO had a rather disconcerting encounter with a former colleague, who told him, "That whole thing has been set up to fail." This was a sobering thought. It meant that some people who might have done great work would not return phone calls when I later inquired about their interest in working at the PBO. And yet, there was also a benefit to the perception that the office was being set up to fail—it spoke to the character of the people who decided to move to the PBO anyway. Perhaps the men and women who took the jobs had grown weary of a government that appeared to be driven on strictly ideological terms. Perhaps they were disillusioned with a civil service that was increasingly prepared to support that type of environment. Whatever their motivations, they would make for a unique and productive dynamic.

What exactly did it mean to be set up to fail? And how could such a strategy be accomplished? After all, the office was newly enshrined within the Accountability Act, an act of Parliament. That meant that it was the law, and the law would have to be respected, right? It couldn't merely be swept under some bureaucratic rug, could it? Senior government officials cannot simply disregard an act of Parliament—can they?

A partial answer involved the funding allotted to the new agency. Compared to similar offices around the world, the PBO budget was woefully inadequate. By tying a funding rope around the neck of the PBO, the government could effectively drag it any way it chose. At least, that is my interpretation. It seemed as if we were expected to behave like children from the Victorian age: we should be seen but not heard.

In addition, the PBO had a large mandate: it was to serve *all* members of Parliament, including the executive branch and governing party. Given that our mandate was so big, it became blurred and out of focus for many. Just exactly what was the overriding mission? Whom would the office primarily serve, and in what capacity? These were questions that had to be answered, given that the PBO was a brand new player on the Hill, and they were the product of relatively weak debate on the Accountability Act. There was little effort to understand the role of legislative budget offices in other countries and the potential benefits for Parliament and Canadians. For the opposition parties, leaving things vague would allow individuals to shape the operating culture. For the government, my sense is that expectations were low. A small office with a big mandate would not be able to go toe-to-toe with big analytical departments such as finance.

The plan to create a PBO had started out as a call for accountability by a party in opposition, a worthwhile idea that should have been of great benefit to all concerned. Underfunded, confusingly structured, and physically scattered around the Library of Parliament, the PBO appeared ready for burial in a sea of bureaucracy. And who would really know or care? What was a skeptical public and press corps to make of such a position? Consider the timing and context of this new office. Many Canadians were frustrated by what had just happened with the

Liberal sponsorship debacle. The average Canadian back then (and probably now, for that matter) would have found the idea of the government creating a new agency rather boring and inconsequential. Who would care about yet another government appointment that, for all a typical Canadian citizen knew, might have been created so that somebody's brother-in-law could get a job?! There had been a growing apathy about all things governmental among the general public, and with good reason. There likely still remains a significant portion of the Canadian population that has no idea what the Parliamentary Budget Office is, let alone what it's supposed to do. Thus, the government probably felt that there would be no rush to resuscitate the PBO if it were put to rest sometime down the road. But in the meantime, a campaign promise had been fulfilled.

Given those circumstances, taking a job in the PBO was unappealing to many of the top civil servants working in Ottawa at the time. And although I have never considered myself someone who goes looking for a fight, eventually I decided to throw my hat into the ring. But getting to that point had been no simple journey. My life had been shaped by many factors, going back to my childhood, and those influences would greatly determine my actions as the PBO. And one single event, more than anything else in my life, would dramatically change me, and give me the courage to tackle this new position of parliamentary budget officer.

TWO

A NORTHERN BOY

My last name is actually Paicz, not Page. It has its origins in Poland and my paternal grandfather, Michael Paicz, brought that name with him when he arrived in Canada in the early 1920s. At that time, there was little or no work to be had in my grandfather's native country. World War I had only recently ended and the future looked dim for all those young people from Europe who could not find jobs. And so, Michael Paicz decided to move to Canada, a country with a lot of wide open space and, from what he had been told, hope and opportunity. However, being an immigrant from Europe also meant a certain degree of social limitation, to put it politely. People felt the need to fit in to their new surroundings, and one way to minimize difference was through a name change, so modifying and anglicizing the family name became commonplace across North America. As a result, although Michael Paicz had gotten onto the boat, Michael Page was the man who stepped off of it. Soon after my grandfather arrived in Canada, he married a young woman from what was then Czechoslovakia. They would have three children, the eldest of whom was my father, James Page. Both of my mother's parents were from Ukraine, which means that we have deep Slavic roots on both sides of the family tree.

For some reason, my grandpa decided to head to the north-western part of Ontario, ending up in a town situated on Lake Superior, one of the biggest bodies of fresh water in the world. The area often referred to as "the Lakehead" originally comprised two cities: Port Arthur and Fort William. In 1970, they amalgamated and became one city, known today as Thunder Bay. But back in the early 1920s, Port Arthur and Fort William were still independent municipalities, and it was in "the fort" that my grandfather attempted to put the hardships of Europe behind him and new hope in front of him. There, pulp and paper mills were being built; mines were being surveyed, staked, and developed.

Over time, the waterfront at the Lakehead had become home to the monstrous grain elevators that began appearing as early as 1882 and now dominated the shoreline. At first they were constructed out of wood; these big wooden cribs were susceptible to fire and many would burn to the ground, only to be rebuilt again and again. Eventually steel replaced wood, and after the turn of the century, reinforced concrete became the new standard for the building and renovation of those enormous structures. Dust from the grain made them dangerous places to work, and more than one employee fell victim to the explosions that often occurred inside the bellies of those beasts. As a kid growing up in the area, I often marvelled at the hugeness of those buildings. Whenever I got close, I would look up at the concrete giants and imagine them as some kind of Northern Ontario equivalent to the Egyptian pyramids, which we read about in school. It was from those grand structures that men would load huge shipments of grain that had come from out west to be stored. Tonnes of wheat and barley and rye could be accommodated at the head of Lake Superior, then wait for transport along the waterways all the way out to the Atlantic Ocean. Those lakers would find customers in all parts of the world.

Life was pretty good for the flood of immigrants that had landed at the Lakehead. They were a true multicultural Canadian mix: Italian, Chinese, Finnish, Swedish, French, Polish, and Ukrainian. But then an economic downturn hit. The Paiczes had left Europe behind in an attempt to escape hardship, only to land in a foreign place just in time to experience the Great Depression. Suddenly there were too many men for too few jobs. If you were lucky enough to land something, it was often in the form of physically punishing labour. Men were expected to work eight to ten hours a day, often seven days a week, with only a half hour for lunch and no coffee breaks. If you didn't like the terms, you were free to move on. After all, there were plenty of others waiting in lines outside those grain elevators and shipyards more than willing to take your spot. They would stand there every morning looking for any kind of work, waiting for someone to falter, get sick, or get fired. They didn't come with résumés or calling cards. Rather, the ones with initiative would stand with a lunch bucket tucked under their arm as if to say to those in charge, "I'm here, and I'm ready to shovel—right now and all day long." My grandfather would take on various jobs through the years in order to support his brood, including working on the railway, but it was a struggle. My family was made up of tough people. They were survivors. They made it through. It was a hard-working, hard-drinking, hard-fighting existence, and if you could keep up, you got yourself a paycheque. With that money, a person could rent an apartment and provide the meat, potatoes, and bread that went on the table of the average northerner.

When World War II broke out, my father tried to enlist but found out that he was too young to head overseas. So, at the age of fourteen, he took a job at the old Canada Car plant, now Bombardier, so he could help his family make ends meet. My dad's younger brother and sister would always look up to him as someone who could make a way for the Page clan in even the most difficult of times.

My father married Stella Manryk in 1951 and the couple eventually had three children. I was the middle child, with my sister Karen born three years before me in 1954 and my brother Bobby three years after me in 1960. Whenever I think of my parents, two things immediately come to my mind: their honesty and their work ethic. Neither had had access to the benefits of a lot of formal classroom education, yet both were intuitively intelligent people who cherished the idea of a substantive education for their children. In addition, they raised us to believe that service to others was important. The notion of helping other people—be they family or strangers in need—had real meaning, especially for my mother.

My mom was always the central pillar of our family, the one we all leaned on, and the single most important person to shape my life. She was very principled, always concerned about the well-being of her family and those who were a part of her circle. She never really cared what we did for a living, but wanted us to know how important family was, and again, wanted us to appreciate the need for service to others. Mom always spoke Ukrainian to my grandparents and had been raised in a Ukrainian culture. She was the one who managed the home and the finances. Dad would make the money but Mom would tend to it! She cultivated a large garden, and with that and the food that was hunted and fished and the berries that were picked, we ate like kings. Mom was also the disciplinarian in our household, and you didn't want to mess around with her rules. One of those rules involved swearing—which was strictly taboo. Once when I was perhaps twelve or thirteen years old, I had just stepped down off a bus after an out-of-town hockey game with my team. My mom was there to greet the bus, and somehow she must have heard me mutter a swear word to one of my teammates, perhaps "Oh shit, I have to do my homework for school tomorrow," or something like that. I didn't know she'd heard anything until the moment I got home and stepped through our front door, when out of the blue came an open hand slap right across the side of my head. It nearly knocked me over. My mom looked at me with a mixture of disgust and anger and said, "Don't use that kind of language." Despite the occasional flare-up like that, she was fair, firm, patient, and loving.

My father was a physically big man, perhaps six foot two or three in his prime. He worked at a number of different jobs, just like his own father had, at manufacturing plants, at saw mills, or on loading docks. It made him a tough man in many ways. Even at the age of sixty-five, my father was still employed, shovelling heavy potash out of railway cars by hand in order to make a living. He was exceptional with his hands and constructed not only the house we lived in on Arthur Street but also the garage that went with it, a tent trailer that we used for camping, and so on. My father was a perfectionist to a fault whenever he decided to build something. He was also an avid outdoorsman, a passionate hunter and fisherman who sought out the wilderness whenever possible. He put all the skills you might associate with being an outdoorsman to good use as he raised his family. I suppose that we all need to find places that give us peace away from the struggles of daily living, and my father found his in the expanses that were available to the people who lived in the north. In the outdoors he was happiest, and he included my mom in a lot of those experiences.

His family was important to him and where possible he wanted everyone involved in everything, from the oldest to the youngest. I can remember going to my grandparents' place, or they would come to our home on a Friday night or Sunday afternoon, and we would all sit on the lawn chairs that my father and grandfather had made themselves. They would tell stories. They would wear their best clothes and brag about this great country of theirs. Every one of them was genuinely proud and thankful to be a Canadian. Whenever I look at photos from that time or watch old Super 8 film shot at family gatherings back then, I can't help but notice the large amount of meat dishes on the table, and preserves too. My father often would wonder out loud "what the poor people were eating." He never meant that to be derogatory, but rather to acknowledge how lucky we were.

Dad loved telling jokes, but he also had a dark side. Like many northerners of that era, drinking became a problem for him and when he drank, he became very moody; things almost always got nasty. He would become a whole different person when he had a glass of liquor in his hand. My teen years were the worst when it came to Dad's abuse of alcohol. I dealt with it as best I could, usually by trying to avoid him. I should have been a better help to him, but I was still pretty young and simply didn't know how to help my father. He went off track for a long time and it caused great stress to everyone who was close to him—especially my mother. Then suddenly, almost magically, he gave up drinking. He stopped, cold turkey.

It took some time but I eventually discovered the impetus for that sudden change, a convergence of things that grabbed my father by the throat and pulled him away from that alcoholic abyss. First, my sister Karen—widowed at a young age with her baby daughter Christina to raise alone—returned from her west coast home to Thunder Bay to be close to her family. Then, within a year, my sister was diagnosed with schizophrenia, a genetic mental health issue. My mother and father would play an important role in helping my sister deal with her illness and in the life of their granddaughter, and I believe that my dad's love for his daughter and granddaughter played a big part in his decision to give up booze. The overriding factor, however, was my mother. After more than thirty years of marriage, she was at her wits' end. She had quietly spoken to our family priest and to a lawyer, asking both men for advice on how to split from her husband if he didn't mend his ways. Apparently, Mom sat my dad down one night and simply told him to stop drinking or else—and she meant it! The fact that she had gone for that professional advice in advance of the discussion must have made an impact on my father. I don't know if he ever fell off the wagon again, but if he did, I never witnessed it. His life had been changed forever, and in a very positive way.

Years later, at my Uncle Ronnie's funeral in Montreal, my father sat beside me at the reception after the interment and at one point, we were alone. He looked at me and, in a very quiet and humble voice, said, "Kevin, I'm very sorry for all those years I spent drinking." There was a pause as he gathered himself. Then he asked, "Can you forgive me?" It was one of those moments that can't help but stick with you—a father asking forgiveness from a son, a man taking responsibility for his actions. It was no doubt a relief for him to seek forgiveness after all those years, and a great gift for me to be able to grant that request. We never discussed the topic again.

After my dad retired, my parents spent another twelve years together before he died in 2005 at the age of seventy-seven. They were good years, a time when he enjoyed the companionship of his wife and respect from his family. He watched as his daughter, with the help of some wonderful doctors and social workers, stood on her feet again. Karen has a life full of love and support and has been able to enjoy two beautiful granddaughters of her own. My dad was also proud that my brother Bobby became a member of the RCMP. He joined the service at an early age and is now a commissioned RCMP officer, who spent his career in detachments across British Columbia. Bobby and his wife, Brenda, have two big boys, Michael and Ian, whose only flaw is that they are Vancouver Canucks fans. (Go, Sens!)

My father's funeral was held at St. Patrick's Church in Thunder Bay. In my eulogy, I noted that Dad had spent the better part of his life within a few blocks of that church. He was always there and always generous, like the time I had been injured at Fort William Gardens during a hockey game and nearly lost my kidney; my father had volunteered to give up one of his if it would help my chances. He could be humble; my mind wandered back to that apology he had made to me in Montreal. He could also be very encouraging; I remember him telling me once when I was a teenager that he believed I was a gifted young man, and that I needed to use those gifts. And, finally, he was tough, which others apparently knew as well. A few days after the funeral, I was at a Tim Hortons in Thunder Bay, standing in line to buy a coffee. An older gentleman kept looking in my direction and eventually came up to me, stuck out his hand, and asked, "Are you Jimmy Page's son?" I said I was. He looked me right in the eyes and said, "Jimmy Page was a tough bastard. Are you a tough bastard?" Only time would tell if I was or not.

Where you were born and raised should never limit your dreams, yet I have often heard people describe their birthplace as a sort of punishment they simply could not overcome. Big cities like Toronto or Montreal or Vancouver have all the resources and the opportunities, they say. To that, I say, "Humbug!" Thunder Bay, Ontario, is certainly geographically isolated—seven hours' drive east is Sault Ste. Marie; seven hours west gets you to Winnipeg; a little over seven hours south takes you across the United States border close to Minneapolis/St. Paul; and seven hours north you will probably find yourself without a great deal of human company.

I have always been very proud of coming from Thunder Bay. To me, it represents a community of helping hands. It is an area of generally wonderful people as well as great natural beauty. In my travels around the world, I have seen some pretty impressive vistas, whether mountain ranges or oceanfront views, but a summer drive west on Highway 17 from Sault Ste. Marie to Thunder Bay is as magnificent as anywhere I've ever travelled. That highway meanders through such quaintly named communities as Wawa, Marathon, Terrace Bay, and Red Rock, all strung along the top of Lake Superior. Suddenly you become witness to panoramic views of water and beach, trees, wildlife, and sunshine. It's gorgeous territory. That's what we notice now, but for my grandparents and parents, that's not what they initially experienced. They endured long days and hard work and there wasn't a lot of time for sightseeing. Growing up in that northern location made me keenly aware of its dangers. The timber in some places is so dense that if you went off the main highway fifteen minutes' walk inland, chances are you'd never get out. You would lose your sense of time, place, and space very quickly and become hopelessly lost. (Now that I think of it, that's a pretty solid metaphor for the life of a civil servant in Ottawa!) To this day I am very thankful for my northern heritage—the people and the place from which I come. If there is any steel in me, it was fashioned by family and geography. I am a product of the north.

With the big lake on one side of you and nothing but bush, hills, and rugged terrain on the other, there is a comforting kind of isolation. In the bush, the sounds of the wind in the trees, the birds crying, and the water lapping a lakeshore make you aware that you are part of something much bigger. Even alone, I never feel lonely in a forest or heavily wooded area; in fact, I feel totally alive. During my time as the PBO, I once had a cameraman come into my office in Ottawa to set up before a scheduled interview. After a few minutes of conversation, he suddenly looked around the room and said, "This looks as if it could be a very lonely job. I wouldn't want to do it." His statement captured something—that even though you might be in the heart of a big city with millions of people, you can still feel very alone. But isolation is no excuse for failure; opportunity abounds every-where in this country.

THREE
MAKING MY WAY TO OTTAWA

When I eventually left the north, it was to pursue a career in economics. My stops along the way included Simon Fraser University in Burnaby, British Columbia; Lakehead University in Thunder Bay; and, finally, Queen's University in Kingston, Ontario. I had my fair share of struggles along the way but I also got lucky sometimes, like when I married Julia Watson, whom I had met back home in Thunder Bay. I had known for a long time what a good, strong person she was, but I would not see the full force of that strength until years later.

During the time when I was living and studying at Queen's University, recruiters would frequently show up on campus to secure potential employees for various organizations, both private and public. As I got closer to finishing my degree, I began paying more attention to those recruiting events. I wasn't so concerned about whether to get into a corporate environment or a public service job—I just wanted to make some money so we could stop feasting on Kraft Dinner. At one event I met a recruiter named Don Drummond, who was at the time a director in the Department of Finance in Ottawa. He did a tremendous job of depicting a life in public service as meaningful and having great purpose—he saw it as a calling. He convinced me that this would be a very solid career path for someone like me. Don would go on to have a terrific career in public service while establishing himself as one of the pre-eminent economists in Canada. At this juncture in 1980, Don helped me land a position as a member of the civil service in the nation's capital, and our paths would cross again many times in the years ahead.

Working in the finance department as an inflation analyst might not sound like the most exciting job in the world, but there was a lot of work to be done in those days given an inflation rate of approximately thirteen percent at the time. The job represented a solid start for a kid just out of university. I replaced Robert Fonberg in that position, and would meet up again with Fonberg down the road to debate with him when he was the deputy minister at the Department of National Defence. We would be discussing the F-35 fighter plane purchase.

My first boss was Munir Sheikh, a tough guy to work for and very demanding, but someone of absolute integrity. A first-generation immigrant from Pakistan, he was a brilliant man who led by example and I consider myself fortunate to have been mentored by such a principled person. Munir would eventually ascend to what he had always described as his dream job, namely, chief statistician of Canada. Unfortunately, he would later feel compelled to resign that posting to protest the government's decision to cancel the long-form census. Munir felt it was vital that Statistics Canada continue the long-form process in order to maintain a viable longitudinal database for the country. Stephen Harper's Conservative government disagreed. Rather than compromise on that issue, Sheikh resigned, leaving with his dignity and integrity intact. At the same time, weak-kneed civil servants stood by and watched as Munir took a lot of heat all alone. Worse yet, some of his colleagues hung him out to dry.

How Munir was treated still bothers me to this day. Munir was right on the long-form census issue, and it was easy for me to say so at committee when the issue came up. History will prove him right. It was also easy for me to highlight Munir's integrity to young public servants around the issue of public service renewal.

As my career unfolded, I held several postings in all of the major sections of the civil service. Between 1982 and 1990, I worked in the finance department, at one point assisting in providing fiscal forecasts under Peter DeVries—Canada's undisputed fiscal guru for several finance ministers. There would be several other stops, including fisheries, agriculture, human resources and social development, and the Privy Council Office (PCO). Among his many accomplishments, Mel Cappe was at one time the Clerk of the Privy Council, and when I moved to the Ministry of Agriculture from the PCO, it was Mel who quipped: "When you are working in the Privy Council Office, you have people who will snipe at you, so you really have to watch your back. When you go to agriculture, you really have to watch your step." He was a diplomat and comedian all rolled into one! I ended up having quite a tour of Ottawa. With that kind of job diversity, I always had a lot of interesting variety in my work. Certainly, I didn't have a deep background for something such as fisheries, except of course for the fact that I'd caught my fair share of pickerel and trout as a kid fishing with my dad and brother. But the different work environments gave me a broader perspective on how our government and the country function—at least from the perspective of an economist. In 2004, while stationed at the Treasury Board of Canada Secretariat, I interviewed and immediately hired a brilliant young man, Sahir Khan, who had been working in New York for some major players on Wall Street. His expertise had been in turning around failing businesses, and Sahir would go on to do big things in many portfolios within the government of Canada in the years ahead.

Eventually I found myself employed as the assistant secretary of macroeconomic policy under the Clerk of the Privy Council, Alex Himelfarb. I served in that capacity between 2005 and 2007. By that time, I was a senior public servant with twenty-five years' experience.

Life was good for the Page family, and seemed pretty normal on all fronts. We lived in a quiet suburb of Ottawa—Barrhaven—and the rhythm of life was moving along as it always had. Julie and I were in the process of raising our three children: Tyler, our oldest; Jesse, our second son and the middle child; and Chelsey, our youngest and the little girl who rounded out our family. Like all families, we ran into our fair share of problems along the way, but one situation was particularly taxing on my wife and me. During 2003, we learned that Tyler, our seventeen-year-old son, had been experimenting with drugs and now had an addiction problem. Suddenly, "normal" had a big crack in it right down the middle of the family.

There is no easy way to deal with such problems, no easy way to pull your child out from under such a heavy rock. I had seen addiction up close through my father's drinking, but this time it was our son and the scourge of drugs. My father had beaten his addiction, and we were hopeful that Tyler would have his grandfather's strength in this regard. Slowly but surely over the next few years, Tyler pulled himself together and began to turn things around in his life. He enrolled to study heritage stonemasonry at Algonquin College, at the Perth campus location, and he truly loved learning the craft. It seemed that he had been born with not only his grandfather's toughness in overcoming personal demons but also my dad's gift of being able to work with his hands. Things were looking up.

But on Saturday, September 9, 2006, everything changed in an instant. At around two o'clock in the morning, I received a phone call from an officer with the Perth, Ontario, police department. When you get a phone call from a police officer, you naturally hold your breath and hope for the best—perhaps the call is a wrong number; maybe your car has been stolen—but my worst fears turned into reality. The officer informed me that our oldest son, Tyler, just twenty years old, had been in a terrible accident. He and some school friends had been out doing what a lot of kids his age tend to do on a Friday night after a long week of classes—drinking. But the night went on too long and somehow Tyler had ended up walking down a railroad track not far from the school campus. He had been hit by a train. I received a second call moments later from the hospital—Tyler was dead. When I heard that news coming through the phone, I dropped to my knees and screamed so loudly that my neighbour would later tell me I had awakened her from a deep sleep that night. It felt as if a knife had been thrust into my stomach. I had never encountered that kind of pain in my life.

At that moment, my world stood still, and life for me and my family would remain static for a very long time. Nothing would ever be normal for us again. For a parent there can be nothing worse, no greater loss. As time passed, I tried to process what had happened, and both my wife and I went through many phases and changes in attitude and feelings. This may sound odd, and it is difficult to actually write it, but at one point I felt a certain anger toward Tyler. I wondered how he could have possibly put himself into that kind of situation. Why wasn't he more careful with his choices? What was he thinking? How could he be so careless, and what about how his family would be affected by his thoughtless actions? Whenever that stream of conversation came up, Julie would point out that I had behaved much the same when I was Tyler's age. She had witnessed it, so I could not deny it. They were the kinds of activities that those of us in the North Country considered as normal, just a part of the march to manhood way back when. But somehow I had been spared. On many occasions, it could just as easily have been me who might have been taken—but it was Tyler. I've thought a million times since that day in 2006 how much I would give in order to trade places with my boy. I'm told that the confusion and feelings I've held about his death aren't all that out of the ordinary. We all process such events in different ways and at different times, within different frames. Tyler had been fighting some demons for a number of years, and he had been winning the battle. But that night, that one night, he made some bad decisions and paid the ultimate price. You look at the details of such an event and you know that had he just fallen in a direction away from those railway tracks, he would still be with us. But he hadn't. I had trouble coping with the apparent randomness of such things. It haunted me then; it still haunts me.

Many wonderful friends came to share in our sorrow. People I had worked with over the years were there to pay their respects— civil servants, politicians, and neighbours alike. Those acts of kindness helped to sustain all of us in the weeks and months after Tyler's passing. But, if I were to tell you that everything worked out just fine, I'd be fibbing. The strain of trying to cope with Tyler's death was enormous. Each of us internalized the loss differently. This wasn't economics—there was no definitive book to read with a game plan we knew would see us through, or some theory to fall back on. I had no idea how to cope.

My other son, Jesse, and daughter Chelsey attempted to handle the loss of their older brother. A parent tries to comfort, but what can be said? The hurt is so deep. Not long after Tyler's death, Jesse headed out west to Jasper, Alberta. He just had to get away. And Chelsey, not unlike her mother and father, struggled with bouts of depression. All the while you stand by helplessly as a parent, desperate to be able somehow to fix things for your children, but you soon come to realize that you can't. I do believe that the strain on parents is different from the stress felt by siblings in such circumstances. We wanted to know how they were dealing with it, but it was very difficult for them to express themselves. Talking about the event often conjured up too much hurt—it seemed that no one wanted to intensify the pain that others in the family were experiencing, so often rooms went silent. We have worried as parents that Tyler's loss will have a lasting legacy, one that might prevent his siblings from living their lives fully. But so far, after an initial enormous emotional hit, there is evidence that both Jesse and Chelsey have been able to cope. Both have completed university degrees, and we are extremely proud of them and inspired by their courage.

My wife Julie showed unbelievable strength. She was coping about as well as anyone could expect, I thought. But the hurt was so great. Slowly, steadily, day by day, the pain began to overtake my wife, and her world started to crash down around her, and us. Her strength ebbed. There were few words. I couldn't help. The strain on a mother who loses a child may be the greatest of all. Julie suffered dearly then and she still does. Like other moms who have lost children, she would often wake up in the middle of the night thinking of our son. So that no one might hear her pain, she would often go into the bathroom, turn on the shower to muffle the sound, and then, as quietly as possible, cry alone. The pain had to be released. But over time, she did find comfort in her network of friends who greatly assisted in sustaining her. She is now part of a group she calls the "crazy ladies," mothers who were brought together by the loss of a child. You might think that they would make depressing company, but that isn't so. They understand each other's pain and do the best they can to lift each other up. They are a sisterhood of compassionate, caring women and they laugh together quite a bit.

I miss Tyler tremendously and always will. I miss the talks, I miss the hope I had for his future, and I miss what he brought to our family. It is a void that can never be filled regardless of all the great things that continue to happen in my life. The hole in my heart is there, every day, and I have come to accept that fact. I don't care how strong a marriage is—in these types of circumstances, a husband and wife will have their problems. Julie and I have had our ups and downs since Tyler's passing, but our mutual respect and love have kept us together and seen us through some trying times. Whenever one of us seems down, the other works hard to be uplifting. The dangerous part is when we are both down at the same time, so we try to first recognize and then avoid those circumstances as much as possible.

The death of a child fundamentally changes who you are on a number of levels. I have said that once you bury a child, not much else can hurt you. Material things don't mean so much anymore. Losing a job seems rather minor compared to burying your son. I say that because all the while the professional clock was still ticking for me. At some point I had to face my work again, my office. We still had to pay the bills. I dealt with the hurt any way I could. People medicate themselves in all kinds of ways when these types of events happen. But eventually, somehow, you must get back to the rhythm of living. Eventually, you must get back to your profession. I decided that work would be the best thing for me and so I returned to my duties at the privy council, where I found myself part of a group of people who provided briefing notes for Prime Minister Harper on a variety of issues. I tried, desperately, to stay tuned in and focused on my job. But the simple truth is that after Tyler's death I was not in a good place on any level, and that included my work. Finally, I asked for three weeks away from the office. During that time I did little other than ride my bike and reflect. Sometimes I would ride a hundred kilometres in a day, going to Tyler's gravesite to sit and wonder at what had been taken from us. On other occasions, I would ride all the way to Perth and walk up and down the tracks near the spot where he had been killed. I walked those tracks dozens of times, looking for anything that might have belonged to Tyler. It was tough letting him go.

After I returned to the office again, it became evident that some people there would prefer that I went elsewhere within the public service. In retrospect, I probably rubbed Kevin Lynch, the Clerk of the Privy Council, the wrong way. Lynch was the boss and he should have the people around him that he wanted. As time wore on, it became increasingly obvious that a change was needed; I knew it, and both the clerk and deputy clerk said that they believed it would be best for me and everyone else at the PCO if I moved on. I was told that I had done a solid job of "managing down"—that is, I had managed those employees I was in charge of, the ones who reported directly to me, just fine. But I was not doing well at "managing up"—helping those above me achieve their career goals. I wasn't playing the game as well as I could, and I suppose I wasn't making them look very good. I received two poor job appraisals in a row, raising issues about my professional performance and attributing them in part to the fact that I had suffered the loss of a child. At the same time, I was questioned on my management of some internal files that may have put me in the crosshairs of the public service senior management group. Had I lost a step after Tyler's death? I probably had. Yes, I was struggling. But I was still a part of some great work being done there. I felt that I was far from finished in my professional career. There was a lot left in the gas tank; I just had to find a way each day to turn the key and start the engine. Eventually I took on a special project at Human Resources and Skills Development Canada (HRSDC) dealing primarily with issues involving governance and the organizational status of Service Canada. But my career was sliding sideways and I knew it. There was not a lot of joy on any level during this time. My life felt like a grind every day, from the moment my eyes opened up until the moment I would close them again, hoping to find some peace through sleep.

While all of this was unfolding, many colleagues and close friends continued to urge me to apply for the newly created position of parliamentary budget officer. I initially bristled at such a thought and would rebuff them all. By this time, I had been a civil servant for twenty-seven years. I certainly didn't need the kind of aggravation that a job like the PBO would almost certainly generate. I was getting to that point in my professional life when I could actually start to envision a winding-down of my career—I could see the finish line if I could just hang on. I was still in the middle of trying to deal with all of the emotional impact of Tyler's death, a personal hell that was not ebbing. Almost every night I would wake up in a cold sweat, often experiencing difficulty breathing. For some reason, I had trouble getting enough air into my lungs and I would have a drowning feeling. Once I knew that sleep was no longer possible, I would get out of bed, sit in a chair in the living room, and try to read a book at three o'clock in the morning. Then I would have to force myself to get out of the chair as dawn approached, head out the front door and try to put a smile on my face and perform my duties at the office. I write these words not in an attempt to elicit sympathy. People across this country deal with similar burdens every day and, in some cases, in even more difficult situations. Still, those were tough times.

Perhaps my friends and family saw something in that PBO position that would serve to strengthen me and give me new purpose. They all must have known it before I did, because I kept receiving encouragement to tackle the new posting. The more I thought about it, the more I realized that, if I was picked by the prime minister to do the job on my last stop as a public servant, it might not be such a bad place to go out. If I was fired, I could live with it. That wasn't heroic on my part; it simply reflected the way I felt, given what had happened to Tyler. I interviewed for the position in December 2007, and I eventually found out that very few truly qualified people even applied for it. Perhaps I won by default. Maybe the prime minister felt that I was the most qualified applicant to be the first parliamentary budget officer given my history as a civil servant. Perhaps he felt I would just do what I was told, based on my résumé at various departments along with the recommendations I must have received from colleagues. Perhaps he thought that, given the turmoil that had occurred in my life with the death of my son, I might not be as vigilant in the position as I might have been, meaning that the Prime Minister's Office (PMO) wouldn't have to contend with any worries coming from the PBO. Or maybe he felt empathy for me and thought the job would be a good fit for all parties concerned. However it happened, in the end the prime minister chose me. I'll probably never know why I received the call. But when that call was made, I accepted the job.

FOUR

AND NOW FOR SOMETHING
COMPLETELY DIFFERENT

My term as Canada's first parliamentary budget officer commenced on March 22, 2008. It came together pretty quickly. Suddenly I had some pressing set-up work to get done. Establishing a brand-new office within an institution such as Parliament would be no easy undertaking.

Two primary objectives had to be met in short order. The first major task was to gain the trust of key players on the Hill. During the first few months in my new position, I made many trips to various locations in Ottawa in order to garner support and gather information. I was introduced to members of different parliamentary committees to whom I would inevitably be reporting. There were consultations with MPs, senators, and other stakeholders in an attempt to determine the best possible operating model for the office. Sometimes meetings occurred in a group setting and at other times in a one-on-one situation, but in each of those meetings, I would listen intently to their suggestions. I needed all the meaningful information I could gather because there wasn't a lot of room for error during the set-up stage.

One particularly memorable meeting was with the finance critic for the NDP at the time, the man who would eventually take over the leadership reins of that party, Thomas Mulcair. He is an impressive person. From the moment we first shook hands, I understood how he had developed his reputation of being a pit bull. When I met him that day, I tried to converse in his native language, French, feeling that I owed him that courtesy. The problem is that my French has never been very smooth. In fact, several of the people I have worked with over the years maintain that having to listen to me speak conversational French can make their ears bleed. But I tried. When I apologized for my lack of linguistic skills, he insisted that I practised a very good "civil service" French. I appreciated his tact. On the flip side, I believe Mulcair appreciated that I made the effort to seek his approval. I needed his kind of authority behind me if the PBO had any chance at all of making a difference. He knew it—and so did I.

I also met the auditor general of the day, Sheila Fraser, on more than one occasion early in my term. I appreciated her candour and remain a very big fan. The credibility of the Office of the Auditor General grew during Sheila's time in the position because of her outstanding leadership. She was visionary in her approach to the office and a great communicator. Sheila talked with me about the importance of a solid business model for our office. She maintained that people needed to be clear about why we would be examining a particular issue. She discussed the importance of an efficient back office so that reports would be professional and timely. But, given our circumstances at the PBO, we could never hope to replicate the business model of the Office of the Auditor General. For one thing, their budget was approximately thirty times larger than ours. And there wasn't much space between our PBO front and back office. We were working out of a proverbial garage. We would have to formulate our own distinct business model.

The second major task was to fill out my staff. I desperately required people who possessed real experience at departments responsible for budgeting (such as finance), to ensure that all parliamentarians would have access to the knowledge, data, and experience needed to carry out their work. This was clearly a part of the mandate as I interpreted the legislation. It is a wise management practice to have succession capability built into any organization, so I also wanted to make sure that we had some bright minds in the group ready to take over once my term was completed at the PBO. At a minimum, the next budget officer should be a person who had worked on federal budgets. In addition, I wanted us to construct a legislative budget office in Canada that followed all of the key principles eventually laid out by the Organisation for Economic Cooperation and Development (OECD), of which Canada was and remains a member. Those principles include elements of independence, transparency, and information sharing. The OECD seeks to provide countries thinking about establishing a legislative budget office with a framework for building something that will deliver value for their legislatures and citizens over time. We wanted legislators in Canada to know that we were following those very principles in protecting the independence of the office; in seeking information to carry out our legislative mandate; and in the way we produced and released PBO documents. On the one hand, these principles would provide us with a level of protection; on the other hand, these principles set a high bar. We were building something new for the country, and we wanted to get it right. Why should Canadians have to settle for anything less?

The philosophy surrounding the office would go deeper than merely a model of operation. Samy Watson, a man who held deputy minister positions at various departments within the civil service, would often ask one question whenever a tough problem confronted any group he was leading: "What is the right thing to do here for Canada?" He didn't want to know about the politically wise thing to do, or what might be the most expedient approach. Rather, he wanted to do the right thing as a civil servant who was acting in the best interests of his country. His example stayed with me, and I wanted that fundamental concept to infuse all aspects of the PBO.

Eventually, I assembled what I considered to be some of the most talented people available for the task. A good hockey analogy might be in order. Imagine for a moment that you had been asked to be the coach for one of those powerhouse Montreal Canadiens hockey teams of the mid-1970s, teams that consisted of such greats as Yvan Cournoyer, Steve Shutt, Guy Lafleur, Larry Robinson, and so on. Once a group like that is in place, your primary duty as the head coach would be to "open the gate"—get out of their way and let them play. And so it was with my PBO team as well. They were brilliant within their respective areas of expertise. But of greater importance was the fact that they all had another quality that counted for more than mere intelligence: they were all *fearless!* They could not be intimidated by anyone, regardless of whether that person had a higher position, rank, or level of authority. These star players are people that you have probably never heard of—but you should. You need to know a bit about each of these players who so dramatically influenced the PBO during my five years in the position. You need to know them because it was that group collectively who did the bulk of the work at the PBO. Without their fearlessness, I very much doubt if many of our efforts ever would have seen the light of day.

Patricia Brown was my first hire at the PBO, in the spring of 2008. She had a wonderful understanding of the workings on the Hill, and was a tremendous organizer and a workhorse. She was my executive assistant, and the type of person that any organization needs if it has a chance of being successful.

Soon after Patricia was hired, senior manager Mostafa Askari joined the team. He was an Iranian by birth, had earned a PhD in economics at Queen's University, and was working at Health Canada as the head of all research when I came knocking. He had also previously run the forecasting division at the finance department, so he possessed an unassailable depth of experience from which to draw. I needed his kind of experience in our office. Over the years in my own assignments within various government departments, it had become apparent to me that youth was often, and increasingly, valued over experience. While youthful enthusiasm certainly benefits any team, experience is invaluable. Mostafa was a veteran public servant who knew the lay of the land. And he was someone that I could trust when the pressure hit.

Shortly after securing Mostafa's services, I persuaded Sahir Khan to join the team. Sahir had been working at the Treasury Board of Canada Secretariat. He was a second-generation Canadian, born to parents who had deep roots in India and were well respected in Ottawa among the public service community. Sahir earned an MBA from Columbia University and had subsequently worked in New York turning around failing businesses for various Wall Street firms. He had an attitude of "go big or go home" from the moment I first met him that has never left him. His counsel was a vital part of our office success given his global perspective on issues. He knew when to ask, "Where is the business case in all of this?" That might sound like a straightforward question, yet the reality was that across various government agencies that kind of basic financial logic was missing. Many times when he'd ask such questions, blank stares were the only response. Sahir would challenge those vacant looks and change many working environments in the process. In the business of public service, Sahir Khan was a superstar—plain and simple.

Next was Harvard-educated Ram Mathilakath, who was brought in to start projects and help with office set-up. Ram grew up barefoot in India, so he had known hunger. He lost a brother in the Indian Ocean tsunami that occurred on December 26, 2004, so he had lived through tragedy. During a time in 2009 when the government was pressuring me to resign, Ram recounted to me how his dad had told him on more than one occasion that honesty, above all else, was the quality he most admired in a man. His father would say, "Be an honest man and if you lose your job I will share my last loaf of bread with you." Ram believed that there is always honour in doing right even if there is perceived personal cost. He helped get me through some difficult times on the Hill.

Then Tolga Yalkin came on board as a senior policy adviser and analyst. Without question, Tolga is *the* most remarkable legal mind I have ever known. In addition he is a renaissance man, the kind of person who possesses interdisciplinary types of expertise. His dedication to public policy issues and his honesty in all things are both admirable and inspirational. While with the PBO he still managed to maintain a full workload as a law professor at the University of Ottawa. It would be Tolga whose work would be so important on the costing of a certain fighter jet acquisition that the government wanted to push through Parliament.

I do not have the space to list everyone who worked at the PBO, but you now have a sense of the kind of quality people who were willing to bring their talents to the new office. They would be my own centurions—but they were soldiers of a different breed altogether. Yes, any successful organization needs its fair share of foot soldiers who can take orders, but I wanted all my troops to be thinkers and contributors—not just shields. In launching a new legislative budget office for Canada, I realized that I had a once in a lifetime opportunity to show the country what it could look like—how we could function at the highest of levels. I also realized that the office would find itself in the middle of some difficult politics. Some of that conflict would come from elected politicians and some of it from public servants. People like Mostafa, Sahir, and Ram were battle ready.

As things got up and running, I was asked to appear in front of both House and Senate committees to provide information on the direction in which we intended to take the Parliamentary Budget Office. There were also questions about my ability to be impartial in the job, given my history at the privy council where I had worked for Prime Minister Harper. Imagine that! It's amusing to think of that perception now, given how acrimoniously things ended up between the Harper government and me. But back then there was legitimate concern that I might put on the blinders and just be a good old boy, doing what I was told and nothing more. No one in the political game was particularly onside with this PBO thing quite yet. Some perceived my job as one where I would be expected to simply "have a nice big cup of shut the hell up" on a daily basis.

But that was a cup that none of us was eager to drink from. We did not intend to merely occupy space in the library while keeping the noise down. We navigated our way through some of those early challenges, all the while continuing to build the foundation of the office. There were many landmines planted in the political landscape that we had to avoid. Some of our people liked to muse that the Liberals were always "measuring the drapes" for Langevin Block. That is the building located directly across from Parliament and it is the headquarters for the executive branch of government in Canada. Both the Privy Council Office and the Prime Minister's Office are located there. After all, there was a minority government in place at the time. One slip and that minority could come crashing down, putting another party in power with a different taste in window treatments, and thus the need for all of those drape measurements. As time went on during my tenure as PBO, I was viewed by some (often people within the Conservative Party) as someone who was working in opposition to the Harper government while somehow favouring the opposition parties. The reality is that—depending on where a given request for information emanated from or given other political implications of the day—the Liberals weren't always backing the PBO horse. Actually, at times it was quite the opposite. If the curtains might have to be put back into storage because of something coming from my office, then the Liberals would show little support. It was reasonable to assume that an office such as the PBO would be walking into a great variety of circumstances given that we were working within the framework of a minority government. But again, those damned drapes are always being measured by someone!

Sahir once noted that Ottawa comprises three major categories of politicians: those driven by naked politics; those driven by principles; and those driven by, for lack of a better word, tribalism. In the latter case, he was referring to those men and women on the Hill who develop a cross-cutting set of relationships, wherein one day they align on one issue but the next day move to another position within another relationship. These people are tough to judge, tough to get a handle on. They might wear blue, orange, red, or any other political colour. And in the middle of all of these dynamics—personal, professional, and political—we were trying to carve out a niche. More accurately, I should say that we were trying to survive.

I looked at our team and recognized a very diverse and intelligent group of self-starters, men and women with proven track records. So how does one motivate such people? That occupied a lot of my mental energy during those early days. We often hear a lot about "the team," but the reality is that most people rarely feel as if they are genuinely a part of one. How do you create that elusive quality of "chemistry" that so many coaches in sports talk about and try to develop within their various organizations? In practical terms, how might you actually get people with healthy egos to function as a real team, not just one in name?

My plan for effective team building was simple: I had to provide them with a *higher purpose* through their work. These were the types of people who sought meaning in association with their jobs. Real accountability was important. Individually, each had to be ready to sign his or her name to the work, the type of work that we all felt had real importance and impact on citizens. That was not the public service norm in Ottawa at that moment. We would eventually have a full-time staff of between twelve and fifteen people with an initial budget of less than $3 million. That was a pittance compared to many other departmental budgets. For example, the auditor general at the same time had a budget of about $95 million. It meant that my team would have to demonstrate star qualities consistently given the workload and the tight funding. In short, we *had* to be a team because there were too few people to pile the blame on. Over time, being small became a blessing in disguise. If we couldn't have scale, we thought, at least we could adapt with speed. You've probably heard the analogy before—a battleship takes a long time to turn, whereas a smaller boat is far more nimble and can escape tight situations through agility and quickness. We were that small boat. The important thing we had to remember initially was that we should never get into a direct battle with anything bigger than ourselves if we could avoid it—just keep up the speed and outrun everybody.

We used peer reviews, many from world-renowned experts and virtually always done pro bono, in order to critique our

methodology. We needed that feedback before we ever attempted
to apply the data to a given job. It really didn't matter what the
topic might be—Old Age Security (OAS), fighter jets, criminal
reform, etc. In addition, we worked in a manner completely
different from any other department in which any of us had ever
worked. We didn't particularly care where the work was done,
whether that was at home, at the office, or on a park bench. The
aim was to complete your portion of a given job in a timely
fashion and at a high level of quality. We rarely had meetings. I
had always disliked meetings because too often they seemed an
excuse for pontificating or brandishing authority for its own
sake. Ours was a small office, so if you really needed to consult
someone or share something, you could just yell out. We didn't
waste a lot of time writing memos as a result. When we did
meet, it was always informal and usually at a nearby Starbucks.
That turned out to be fortuitous since many key media people
hung out at that same Starbucks—people who would follow up
on our reports. It was a very different atmosphere from Parliament
Hill. Perhaps the best indicator of that was when Sahir Khan,
someone who I contend was born in a three-piece suit, started
showing up at the office wearing jeans.

And of paramount importance was the data. Always the data!
Many times, our own government would not provide us with the
information we needed, no matter how much we begged or
threatened. We would therefore have to be creative about how we
secured our data, and Canadians should be concerned to realize
that *we often had to secure our own national data from sources outside of
Ottawa*. For example, to get estimates of Canada's potential output
in the possession of the finance department, we needed to go to
the International Monetary Fund (IMF) based in Washington,
DC. To get information on the costs of running a prison system,
we needed to go to the provinces. We would end up doing a lot

of comparison work with relevant data made available from other countries. If the government of Canada would not hand over reliable information for us to use, then we would draw our conclusions based on the analogies we might derive from outside database sources. One such important source was our friends at the Congressional Budget Office in Washington, but there were many others. Our belief was and remains that superior data always translates into superior reports. Sometimes we would make a simple phone call and connect with a world expert who had specific expertise that we required. At other times we would drop everything, get in a car or on a plane, and visit someone who could supply high-quality data for a specific costing. When it comes to government agencies, both inside and outside Canada, I was always amazed at how many times we would be the first such visitors to seek the data, and more often than not people were happy to oblige. Our office would eventually be recognized by the IMF for the consistent quality of our work.

Everybody had a role to play, whether they were a senior member, a junior in rank, or an intern looking to make a name. Whenever we interviewed people for jobs at the PBO, we would indicate that inevitably they would be identified right alongside me or any other of the senior analysts who worked on specific pieces. If their names were on the cover page of the report, they would have to be accountable for their work. Sahir would often ask candidates if they were ready to "sit at the grown-up table," as he called it, because when the dirt inevitably hit the fan on any given report, people would have to stand up and be counted. An intern might just as easily be sitting at the table right beside me and feel the fire from MPs, the media, and anyone else who wanted a pound of our flesh. Obviously, that isn't for everybody; it takes a special type of person to be able to withstand that kind of working environment.

Internally we discussed the idea that very few government institutions ever garner much attention. Rather, we concluded, it is the people who occupy those institutions whom media will inevitably turn to—the personalities that inhabit the departments and the buildings. And so, we agreed that when it came to making announcements and briefings with the press, I would be the "face of the franchise." "PBO" needed to be more than just an initialism if the office was going to survive and thrive. Whether I wanted it or not, I was going to be front and centre on any major stories that would involve the PBO. We knew that the information game could only be played one way from our end, and that was to ensure that all political sides got the same information all the time. We could not start playing those political games of dishing out bits and pieces to one media entity and other tidbits to a different group. We realized that the press could be a powerful ally in helping to publicize our work and, more importantly, might be able to help us survive!

At that time, the minority Harper government had been in power for about three years. It is worth mentioning that during that time members of the media, especially those situated in Ottawa, had been treated very poorly by the government. Some tough people had been running the show previously in the nation's capital, political staffers who wanted complete control of the flow of all information emanating from the government. But Prime Minister Harper took that desire for ultimate control to a whole new level. It was shutdown time on Parliament Hill and little information was being made available to anyone, let alone the press. Much has been written in recent times about all of the people in "short pants," a reference to the relatively youthful composition of the PMO. Obviously, Prime Minister Harper prefers that dynamic among his staff. My guess would be that his desire to control information is easier to accomplish with young staffers as opposed to a group of veteran politicians. The "short pants" reference came up during the Senate expense scandal, which illustrates that Harper's men and women did not have the prerequisite experience needed to navigate such troubled waters. No, a veteran and politically astute chief of staff within any PMO would have known that you cannot, as Nigel Wright did, write cheques to senators who work on behalf of Canadians so as to hold the executive to account. That goes beyond bad politics—it reflects poor judgment and a lack of experience. I spent many years working at the Privy Council Office, and witnessed firsthand how an experienced person like an Eddie Goldenberg (former prime minister Chrétien's long-time senior adviser) could positively affect a prime minister's leadership. Eddie knew how the town worked and, perhaps more importantly, he also knew *how it did not work.* When the Conservatives took power in 2006, it was heartening to see that the new prime minister had chosen Derek Burney to steer the ship during the transition process. Burney was a terrific choice, being experienced, honest, and tough. Not only did he possess the positive attribute of coming from Thunder Bay (I'm biased in that regard), but he also had a solid résumé that included being the former chief of staff to Prime Minister Brian Mulroney; serving as the Canadian ambassador to the United States; and holding a senior public servant position within the Department of Foreign Affairs. That is the type of person that every prime minister should have at his or her disposal. Before he exited, Burney helped set up the new government and the first Speech from the Throne, and helped craft the first budget. He left with everything in place. It is a shame that Prime Minister Harper has not sought more veteran public servants such as Burney to help run his PMO, which I think reflects poor judgment on the part of the prime minister. He consistently chooses people willing to nod their heads "yes" on command, an apparent reality that has cost the prime minister in recent times in any number of areas. There are just too many "short pants" at one time.

The Harper government has allowed very few people from the various governmental departments to share even minor bits of information with the media. If anyone talks out of turn, they might have to pay a steep price for a perceived lack of loyalty. That mentality has accelerated a feeling of fear from within the ranks of the civil service, and in my own little world of acquaintances and professional affiliations, that reality began to show itself in some unusual ways. Soon after I became the PBO, I began to notice some strange behaviour whenever I would attend a function in the city where politicians and civil servants had gathered. It could be at a charity event—say, a wine and cheese reception where photos were being taken. Many times if I were standing with someone of a particular political leaning (usually Conservative) or with a young public servant hoping for that next promotion, they would suddenly walk away if a photographer happened to get close. No, they wouldn't walk—it would be more like a full gallop to get away from me. It was like the town had been divided up into teams and unwritten instructions were given not to engage those not directly working with or supporting the government. But apparently I wasn't the only poison in town. Many political types in the city became scared even to be seen with certain members of the media. The press was being shut out, the civil service was fearful, and simultaneously the government was trying to muzzle the PBO. Such was the atmosphere that had been created by the prime minister and his leadership group. The vise was tight and getting tighter day by day. It was a concerted effort at a centralization of power and information, the likes of which I had never seen in all my years on the Hill. Everyone in our office knew that this was reality, but we also knew that it could be used to our advantage. Given that the government had decided to go virtually silent, the media would have to gather its data from whatever reliable source(s) they could find. The PBO would become one of the most important information portals available to the media when it came to financial issues on Parliament Hill, if not *the* most important.

As a part of our initial set-up efforts, I (along with two PBO staff members) headed to Washington, DC, so that we might witness firsthand the workings of the Congressional Budget Office on Capitol Hill. Specifically, we wanted to see how our counterpart in the United States had organized its offices. Obviously, theirs was a far bigger undertaking with greater numbers in both personnel and budget. However, that visit was enlightening for our team as the people we met were forthcoming and helpful. We needed input in a broad sense on our mission, a viable business model for operational purposes—even the branding of our new office. Most importantly, we learned valuable lessons about what we had to be mindful of in our roles back home. We gained good information from the deputy director of the CBO at the time, Robert (Bob) Sunshine. Bob was well known in Washington and had gained stature within the civil service community around the world. He understood the challenges we were facing and was more than willing to share his experience with all of us. He offered three pieces of great advice. First, he told us that we had to produce quality analysis day after day. He said that our information would have to be better than any other available data if we were going to build credibility. Second, he said we needed to learn how to communicate with legislators as well as the public. Here was a man whose experience went all the way back to the Richard Nixon administration. He was battle hardened. And as he spoke to this need for excellent communication, I suddenly realized that I had a deficit to remedy in this area. After all, I was a career bureaucrat and as such had never been exposed at great length to dealing with the media or MPs in a very public context. Bob was telling me that I would have to be a quick study in this regard. Third and finally, he said that we would need to be tough. Why? Since the primary function of our office would be to try to make the government accountable, some factions might attempt to undermine us or even get us fired. Bob's comments were prophetic. Here we were in 2008, not yet having written our first report, and someone was telling us that our jobs could be at risk. It was a memorable moment for me as the office of the PBO was being formulated.

We also determined during that trip to Washington that we would need to have our product pipeline up and running relatively quickly. By "product," I mean that, beginning very soon, we would have to produce relevant and significant reports for members of Parliament and all Canadians. Further, those reports would need to generate three or four banner moments per year if we expected to achieve any measure of credibility. And as one product was being completed and delivered, another would have to be developing in that pipeline.

While we were tending to our operational due diligence, the PBO team continued to grow and be strengthened by experienced and talented public servants. One such person was Chris Matier, who left the top forecasting job at the finance department to help build our new legislative budget office for Canada. In short order, Sahir managed to hire both Peter Weltman and Jason Jacques, men who had experience within all of the major budgeting departments such as finance, treasury, and the Privy Council Office. Suddenly, we weren't just a good team—we were becoming a *deep* team as well. In a little over five months, the office had been put together and our work was well underway.

Then, it happened. We were asked by Paul Dewar, member of Parliament for the NDP in Ottawa Centre, to estimate the costs incurred by Canada's engagement in the war in Afghanistan. We would eventually be involved in many high-profile costing projects in the years ahead, but few were more important or more politically charged than our costing report on Canadian military efforts in Afghanistan. Once the request was received by our office, we began obtaining the needed data for costing purposes. Remember, part of the PBO mandate is that it serves parliamentarians, not just the government in power. We were expected to act on requests where we could, given our manpower and budget constraints, so we had to pick and choose which jobs we should undertake. When Dewar's request was received, Ram Mathilakath immediately walked into my office, smiled, and said, "This is the one we've been waiting for!"

FIVE

AFGHANISTAN REPORT AND
THE AFTERMATH

Costing a war is complicated work. It can be a daunting undertaking, even for those fortunate enough to be in possession of all the necessary information to complete the task. We had a great group willing to tackle the job, but our numbers were few. Still, we realized the importance of the project and concluded that yes, this could be done. Our task wasn't made easy by our own federal government, which provided us with cursory data from which we could do only a portion of what we intended to accomplish. They did give us some information on troop deployment needed to assess the actual costs of operations on the ground, but it wasn't enough. We needed more numbers so that we could provide complete, real-time costing. Our objective was to include everything related to the engagement, including costs of the boots on the feet of our soldiers; the value of capital deployed in the theatre of war such as helicopters, transport vehicles like jeeps, tanks, and weaponry; developmental aid; and finally, death and disability costs as well.

We sought and received estimate numbers from the Australians, the British, and the Americans, who were also engaged in Afghanistan. We spent the most time speaking with our American counterparts on this issue. Specifically, we worked through the

Congressional Budget Office and its Congressional Research Service for costing methodologies for operations, capital, and veterans' issues—what not to include, what to include, and how to include it. Unlike Canada, U.S. officials had already provided their legislatures with figures in this regard. Our American colleagues were very open and helpful, and with their assistance we were better able to understand how costing was done in other jurisdictions, such as the United Kingdom and Australia. We wanted to give our legislators information that was authoritative and comparable with the quality of estimates already provided in other countries. It would not be the last time that other governments or experts from around the world would help the PBO once our own government had decided to go silent.

During the research and writing of that report, news surfaced that the Canadian death toll in Afghanistan had reached one hundred soldiers. Like most Canadians, we read those headlines and grieved. Our work took on even greater meaning, as it wasn't just about the numbers—it was about the people who were represented by those numbers. Everybody involved in that project picked up the pace.

In September, I did an interview with Global TV and discussed such topics as the PBO and war costing. That raised a few eyebrows on the Hill, where the idea that the PBO was supposed to be an independent, transparent operation hadn't really taken hold. By this time, Sahir and his team had partially constructed a website where everything that we produced would be located in plain sight. Anyone could read it and learn about our methodologies and the projects they served. Again, more eyebrows were raised. How could a civil service entity go public with what had historically been perceived as sensitive information about current issues? It just wasn't done on the Hill. But we did it. The website featured all aspects of our operations: every communication, every paper, and every piece of correspondence. There would be no hiding. All of it was put on that website. That was part of the twenty-first-century operating model we had envisioned, one in which there would be no secrecy. It was also an insurance plan of sorts: publish the best analysis we could and stand behind the results. We had decided to create and implement a transparent, accountable, analytical, and lean public sector organization, and all of us at the PBO felt that we were simply fulfilling our mandate.

We released documents containing all kinds of information, including consultations and our business model, for all to see. It liberated us in that it meant we didn't have to play games as to which reports would be posted and which were too sensitive for public consumption. We did the work and then posted the results for everyone to examine and critique. The concept of transparency—*genuine, real transparency*—had meaning for all of us. Canadian taxpayers were footing the bill so we believed they should have access to our work. But then we ran into a dicey situation as the time grew near to release our findings on the costs of the Afghanistan mission. Canada's fortieth General Election had been called and was to be held on October 14, 2008. This meant that Parliament was effectively shut down. It looked like we would have to sit on the report until after the election, but the heat was being turned up on the government by the media to make the report public. All of the political leaders were repeatedly asked questions about our impending report during the various stops along the campaign trail. Eventually, the leaders of all the opposition parties made their play, demanding that the document be released right in the middle of the election campaign. It was an unprecedented request, and if we agreed to it, there were many practical and political implications for the PBO. The only way that any release could happen was if *all* parties agreed to it, meaning that Prime Minister Harper would have to join with party leaders Gilles Duceppe of the Bloc Québécois, Jack Layton of the NDP, and Stéphane Dion of the Liberal Party in giving approval. Surprisingly, the prime minister did indeed agree. However, sensing his trepidation, I hesitated. His endorsement hadn't sounded all that genuine. We had to be careful because we could be held up for some awful bashing if we didn't do the right thing on this issue. There was a lot of internal debate over the topic of "release or don't release" the report. Again, we tried to arrive at a decision without worrying about its impact on our "survivability." If this was going to be our first and last document, if this would bring down the operations of the office, then so be it. We all decided that we'd make it one hell of a document on our way out the door. But then, for a second time, Prime Minister Harper said publicly—and in more convincing tones— that the Afghanistan report needed to be released in order to assure Canadian voters that there was nothing being hidden. The decision to release the report suddenly became much easier.

It was politics at its most visible in Ottawa—the opposition leaders forcing the hand of the prime minister to the point where he had to let the report go public, lest he be hounded for the rest of the campaign about its contents. Being perceived as secretive in an election campaign is not what *any* politician wants, let alone the person who is the head of a minority government. It was during this time that I encountered the Clerk of the Privy Council (and my former boss), Kevin Lynch, at a function for CANARIE, the organization that runs Canada's research internet backbone and that had been cofounded by Lynch himself and Rafiq Khan, Sahir's father. On that occasion, Lynch mentioned the upcoming release of the Afghanistan report and cautioned us to "make sure it's good." That implied to me that he was speaking for the group of people he repre-sented in the public service. The stakes were high.

Here is what we knew. Our report contained key informa-tion that detailed four vital parts to our national involvement in Afghanistan. First, we wanted to know what the differences in costs would be for housing a soldier in Afghanistan versus a location on our home turf—say, Petawawa, Ontario. We looked at monies spent on items required to keep our soldiers on the ground in that region of the world for a year, which included items such as food, salaries, clothing, and so on. Our estimate was approximately $675 000 to $765 000 per soldier deployed per year (depending on the year). Of course, we couldn't compare our operational estimates to any figures produced by the govern-ment because they never provided such numbers.

Second, we put together a dollar amount for capital depreci-ation. This included the wear and tear and loss of hard assets we had on the ground, from aircraft to tanks to jeeps and so on. We estimated annual depreciation costs in the $1.5 billion to $2 billion a year range in the later years (assuming four to eight percent of the Department of National Defence's capital assets were deployed, and accelerated depreciation because these assets were in a theatre of war). Again, the government never produced a comparable type of estimate.

Third, we felt compelled to supply estimates for death and disability costs for our troops. Based upon available data, we projected costs within a range of between $1.5 billion and $3 billion in this third category. And what was the government's range for this category? You guessed it—they provided no estimate. This is deplorable because there should have been a debate early on to ensure we were going to set aside sufficient funds to help the families of deceased soldiers and meet the needs of physically and emotionally wounded veterans.

Fourth and finally, there was money being spent on the development aid side for building institutions in Afghanistan such as schools, hospitals, and water filtration systems for when the war would eventually subside. Our number for this came in at about $1.7 billion.

One last point is worth a mention here. Based on our research, we estimated that Canada's total expenditures related to the war from 2001 to 2011 were in the range of $14 billion to $18 billion. At that time, government did not provide mission-specific estimates for the various departments, whether it was the DND, Veterans Affairs Canada, or the Canadian International Development Agency (CIDA).

Our office had the key costing parts for the report in pretty good shape, but we were still not yet ready to release our findings. Another seven to ten days were required in order to get it all put together and ready for distribution, but we were running out of time. We needed every hour right up to the final day to finish our work. It was all hands on deck to put the document in a professional form that could be both read and understood by all who received the package. We also needed to have it translated into French. We asked the resource people at the Library of Parliament to help, but they said it couldn't be done in a week. No problem. We called John Allaire of Spin Communications, and asked what he thought. His response was, "I don't need to sleep; it will be done." We needed that kind of attitude because this was a key moment for all of us at the PBO: hit a home run and we would have instant credibility; strike out and we would be nowhere.

We had also contracted a company called BlueSky Communications to assist us in setting up the release as efficiently as possible. Among other things, they organized the location, sent out the press release to the media and other affected parties, and prepped me for what would be my first and only press conference during my time as PBO. Yes, I've heard and read some comments from those who thought I held too many pressers in my time as PBO, but the truth is that the October 8, 2008, event was the only real press conference I ever held. There were very good reasons to do so. Every other report that was released through my office was done first for MPs, followed by a separate briefing for media and experts. Sometimes members of Parliament would show up, but more often than not there was never a big turnout from that group. But trust me, the media would always show up. They knew how to follow a scent. The BlueSky people ran me through a series of questions in a mock press conference set up the day before the event. I went through the practice session as best I could and then something interesting happened. I looked over at Mostafa once the mock presser had been completed, and he didn't look happy. I asked him how he thought it had all gone. He looked at me and said, "Kevin, forget the script and what they have on paper for answers. Just be yourself. You know that report better than anyone, with the exception of the authors. Go in with the numbers and then just be authentic." It was great advice from someone who knew me and knew what we all needed the next day. That was the end of my formal training session. The rest of my training would come from on-the-job experience and talking to veteran media people like journalist James Travers over one of our lunches.

Many of the team members at the PBO stayed up the better part of the night to make sure that everything was in order. Pat Brown insisted before the big day that I go home and get some sleep, but after she kicked me out, Pat ended up staying there all night herself. Sahir, Ash Rajekar, and Ram kept revising to ensure the document was ready. Even up to the very last moments, they were inputting the feedback from the review panel. Also there was Renée St. Arnaud-Watt, a retired public servant with decades of experience at the Privy Council Office who was hired to be an editor of the French translation but ended up being a primary editor of the entire report. I headed out of the office around midnight for home—but never slept more than a few winks. Roger Soler, one of our analysts, actually drove to Kanata in the middle of the night to get CDs burned in order to hand them out to the media the next morning. We got it all done literally moments before we were to go public.

The next day brought beautiful weather to Ottawa—overcast but no rain. It was a great day for a stroll down Sparks Street. My team had assembled at the press conference location very early and I was to join them just before the event was to begin. Everything was in place. I began the four-block walk from our offices at the Sun Life building to where the press conference would be held. As I walked, I thought that this must be what an Olympic moment feels like for an athlete—you just get the one shot. That idea didn't allow me any great comfort. I kept telling myself that I could not screw this up. I wasn't so worried about looking like an idiot in front of the assembled masses, since it wouldn't have been the first time. What I really feared was letting the team down. It had been determined by everyone at the PBO early on in our mandate that we needed a face of the franchise and here I was, about to become that face in a big way. It wasn't something I was particularly looking forward to, especially given that during my years as a civil servant I had remained in the background. But the spotlight was about to be directed right at that bald head of mine whether I liked it or not. All I could do was put one foot in front of the other and keep walking to the location. My stomach was tied up in knots. I noticed the throng of people coming and going from a nearby Tim Hortons and in an instant the words came back from that other Tim Hortons in

Thunder Bay not so long ago—"Are you Jimmy Page's son? Jimmy Page was a tough bastard. Are you a tough bastard?" I couldn't help but smile at the memory, and all I kept thinking was, "I guess we're going to find out soon enough."

I was about three blocks into the trek when I found myself directly in front of the magnificent National War Memorial. I saw a bench directly across from that great edifice, stopped walking, and sat for a moment. My mind grew very quiet as I stared up at the memorial, contemplating all of those soldiers who were so beautifully represented there—past, present, and future. How fitting it was that I would be at that place at that moment, on my way to present a report about our military operations in Afghanistan. And I thought of all those men and women wearing our uniform in that faraway country at that moment, stationed halfway around the world, risking life and limb in service to the country. I knew the contents of our report forward and backward. I also knew that the men and women in our armed forces would not be let down in any way as a result of what we were about to present, since part of our findings would challenge parliamentarians and all Canadians to set aside the necessary resources for our military, whether abroad in harm's way or at home in recovery. "We will honour you this day," I thought.

Just before leaving the memorial I found myself thinking about my late son, Tyler. I stayed there, frozen in place, for quite a long time. I thought of how I missed him, of what we'd all lost, and about how difficult it had been to make our way as a family after his passing. I suddenly knew that if I had been able to get through that event in my life, I could surely make it through a press conference. As I finally began the last leg of my walk, I had a sense of calm that gave me great confidence and strength. I felt Tyler beside me.

When I walked into the Government Conference Centre across from the Château Laurier, I could immediately sense a buzzing excitement. Adding to that atmosphere was the building itself, a very impressive backdrop for any kind of gathering in Ottawa. Originally a railway station, with hallways soaked in history, it was in that very building that former prime minister Pierre Elliott Trudeau negotiated the repatriation of our Constitution with the provinces. Conference Centre protocol is that a lockdown occurs whenever a major piece of government information is going to be distributed to members of Parliament and the press and serves as a sort of "time out." Whoever comes into the briefing area cannot leave before anyone else. This means that there can be no leaks to any outside agency, no story written, no policy contemplated before the information is presented in full and in an organized fashion. As I entered, the lockdown was already underway.

I was met by Sahir and Mostafa and taken to a room adjacent to where the press conference would be held. The press had already received the report and I was informed that the initial reaction had seemed relatively positive. "That's good news," I thought. But then as I looked over at those two men, I had a sudden sense of uneasiness. Neither had to say a word—I knew exactly what they were thinking because their faces gave them away: "Can this guy handle it? Can he get the job done?" I answered those unspoken questions in my own mind—"Well, gentlemen, let's go find out." As I made my way into the briefing room, the last thing I heard was Sahir's voice as he asked one of the BlueSky people, "How many networks are here?" The answer came back; "Five." "Is that good?" Sahir shot back. "We only have five networks in the country" was the response. And with that news still ringing in my ears, I flashed a thumbs-up sign to my colleagues and then stepped into the lights. The team members who were standing off in the wings as I walked into the press gathering said that all they could hear was the steady clicking of cameras for what seemed like an extended period of time. I remember seeing some flashes but not much else. I was focused and ready to report our findings.

I was positioned at a table located directly in front of a series of Canadian flags hanging behind me. "Those BlueSky people know what they are doing," I thought as I settled into my chair. And then I began to read from my notes. I described what we had found in our research in what I hoped was plain language that everyone in the room, indeed everyone in the country, could understand. Certainly, the country had never seen this kind of peer-reviewed document—and never one reported in such circumstances. We had utilized two Canadians and two Americans on that review panel and those experts had given us the green light on what we were reporting. We knew our numbers were pretty close to the mark. We would cover all costs, but we wanted to focus on the cost of disability payments in the years ahead. We have unfortunately been witness in recent times to some of the extreme manifestations of post-traumatic stress disorder (PTSD), including suicide among our returning veterans. The associated costs are real and need to be calculated. We wanted everything transparent and believed that everyone needed to know those costs because they would affect the quality of life for our men and women in the military upon their return to civilian life. And inevitably, on a more macro level, associated costs would also determine the kind of military we would have at the end of this particular conflict abroad. We owed it to our soldiers.

Instead of simply briefing ministers, we were briefing parliamentarians and all Canadians. When the question-and-answer time began, I felt very calm, very assured in what we had produced, so the questions were not difficult to handle. At one point about halfway through the Q&A, a reporter asked, "Are you afraid of retribution for this report?" I assume the questioner was raising the issue that the government would not like the report because it examined costs that had not been disclosed to Parliament. If we made the government look bad, it was possible that there could be negative implications for my job. After all, I worked at the pleasure of the prime minister. I looked at her and instinctively responded to her question with a question of my own, "Do I look afraid?" Then I noted, "I promise you, I'm not afraid." And I wasn't. Believe me that it wasn't said to make me look like some kind of civil service cowboy; I'm not that quick. No, I actually just wanted to know if I looked nervous. But I could hear some chuckles, and Mostafa would tell me later that for him it had been the line of the day. You could see that the press was happy and relieved to ask questions and actually receive clear and pointed answers to those questions.

As the proceedings wrapped up, we all knew that we had done well. We were exhausted but exhilarated at the same time. All of us in that PBO group headed back to the office, turned on television sets, and then watched as the news reports started to air. Liberal opposition leader Michael Ignatieff was responding on one network while New Democratic Party leader Jack Layton was on another. We were watching in real time the power of the pen and power of the press. Was some of the information we provided politicized that night? Probably, but that is on the politicians, not the people who wrote the report. Did the media apply their own particular version of events from the briefing? Undoubtedly, but we didn't write their stories for them either. We had done our job and how the politicians or media chose to use that information was up to them. Shortly after we finished, I received a text from John Allaire, the man who had completed all the document preparations for us. He said, "When you asked that reporter, 'Do I look afraid?' I cried." I think it was a cry for standing up. For the record, John Allaire is one tough guy by any standard. Many people, some of whom we could not have imagined, had become totally invested in this day. Years later, Patricia Brown, my first hire as PBO, would say that the Afghanistan report stood out in her mind as a kind of "top of the mountain moment" for her while at the PBO. Looking back, it's tough to argue with her assessment. But we would have many more memorable moments as a team in the months and years ahead.

As the evening went on, I took a moment and left the group as they continued to watch the various TV accounts. I went to a nearby vacant boardroom, closed the door, and called my wife. As soon as she picked up the phone she blurted out, "It's all over the news. Your team is the lead story tonight; it's on every channel. How did you do it?" I told Julie that I didn't really know how we had pulled it off. Throughout the whole day I had maintained a sense of calm and focus I'd rarely experienced. I told her that I believed that somehow our late son Tyler had been with me the entire time. Somehow he had joined me on the walk over and he never left my mind. I've never been one who cries a lot, but after I'd finished speaking with Julie, sitting there by myself, the tears just began to flow. I suppose it was a combination of things. Stress; relief; joy. We had been advised by the Clerk of the Privy Council to make sure it was good. It had felt better than good.

We learned from this first report that we were going to have to be vigilant in explaining the relevance of independent financial analysis. This would be a labour of love for staff at the PBO. Sometimes challenges would come from the complexity of the work and the professional jargon that could limit audiences. Sometimes challenges would come from political participants and experts who did not like the conclusions of the analysis or the attention it was getting. Whatever the challenge, it really didn't matter—we had to keep selling the benefits of our work one way or another.

Not long after releasing the Afghanistan report, I remember watching a TV interview with retired Major General Lewis MacKenzie, a Canadian hero who served his country and the United Nations with great distinction in peacekeeping missions all over the world. In the interview, MacKenzie was asked what he thought of the PBO costing. He replied as a soldier should, and noted that when he was at war he wasn't thinking about the cost of gasoline as he sent troops to the front line. I took that to mean that a general should focus on the mission's larger purpose, not worry about financial stability when lives are in jeopardy. Our military leaders need to be able to deploy our men and women in uniform with the utmost confidence, knowing that adequate funding will be provided both on the battlefield and when the soldiers return home. But we need our political leaders to be aware of the costs of war, costs that will drive tough political decisions. Questions will be asked from both sides of the House. For example, after more than a decade of military engagement, what kind of military do we want and need? Will we plan for the eventual replacement of all the military equipment that has depreciated very quickly in the sands and mountains of Afghanistan? Will we set aside sufficient funds to ensure that our men and women have access to the care they need to deal with the physical scars and emotional battles that might lie ahead? These are political decisions that should matter to everyone, including retired Major General MacKenzie. Financial analysis matters to our military in many practical applications, but most importantly, it reflects upon the nation's respect for its heroes.

The Afghanistan report represented an early high water mark for everyone at the PBO. Unfortunately, however, all good things must come to an end. Shortly after the Afghanistan report was made public, it was announced that our budget was going to be cut by over $1 million. It was a hard right-cross to the chin of our entire staff, and the start of about a twelve-month low, a period that I can only refer to as "the valley floor." We began to take a lot of hard hits and they continued for what seemed like an eternity. In my opinion, that first blow—the recommended budget reduction—reflected political and bureaucratic anger toward the PBO because of our analysis on Afghanistan. We had provided information that was contrary to the government's depiction of how the war was being run and financed, and we were being punished for going public. We had used a transparent approach to collect, deliver, and publish our findings and that may have been an embarrassment to the government and senior public service personnel—at least from the perspective of those supporting the Conservative agenda. The government wanted to tighten the vise on our little office and bring us into line by attempting to slash our budget. Once that news went public, the press picked up on it in a big way. I would eventually do network interviews with CBC hosts George Stroumboulopoulos and Anna Maria Tremonti, among others, trying to express what we were attempting to do at the PBO. I also wrote to the leaders of all the parties and informed them that the budget restrictions about to be imposed on our office would make the PBO unsustainable. At one point I let it be known that if that budget cut occurred, I would have to close the office. I don't know if I actually could have done that, but it sure got some attention. It was the cry from the press and the push-back from opposition members that kept us alive over those critical twelve months. We slowly pulled ourselves up from the valley floor, all the while keeping our primary goal in view: we had work to do and restrictions on our funding would not, at least in the short term, put an end to it. I suppose the government simply wanted things to remain as they had been for years on the Hill. They wanted to maintain normalcy. But in the words of the great Canadian musician Bruce Cockburn—the trouble with normal is that it always gets worse.

On October 28, 2008, I received a letter signed by Peter Milliken, the Speaker of the House of Commons, and Noël Kinsella, the Speaker of the Senate. That letter, followed closely by a couple of really acrimonious committee meetings, represents the lowest of the low moments during my time at the PBO. It was difficult to confront the animosity directed toward us by some of the committee members. That said, I was always amazed by how calm every member of my team remained even in the most difficult of circumstances—they seemed to possess nerves of steel. The letter in question had been forwarded to the PBO by the parliamentary librarian, William (Bill) Young, and although the letter was signed by the speakers, I have always wondered whether the parliamentary librarian had actually written it. That communication was both terse and foreboding, saying in no uncertain terms that the PBO should basically mind its place. According to the letter, I had a problem with chain of command, not least in the eyes of our prime minister. At that moment I realized in very concrete terms the lengths to which the government would go to keep us in check. I understood that the job of parliamentary budget officer was not going to turn out the way I had envisioned. Apparently once our report on the costing of the Afghanistan war had gone public, it was game on. How dare anyone put information on a website for public viewing! It appeared that all government-related information needed to be contained and released only as the government saw fit. Their belief was that in my role as PBO, I should simply follow the existing practices of the Library of Parliament. The parliamentary librarian was protecting territory and the speakers were acting as the messengers. In my mind, none of them had any vision for what the PBO could do for the country or how its mandate needed to be executed.

It was not my first run-in with the two speakers. I had been told by both of them during separate meetings in the spring of 2008 that I should keep my head down. During another meeting with the government house leader, Peter Van Loan, he noted that there probably wouldn't be much interest in any analysis emanating from a fledgling entity such as the PBO. At first I wasn't quite sure how to interpret these comments. Was I being told not to do the job as well as I could? Was I being warned that I could get my head taken off in a partisan crossfire? But once I read the October 28 letter in detail, I understood that key people wanted me to stay away from the big financial issues of the day and basically do inoffensive work. It looked as if I should focus on items such as private members' bills and other similar, less controversial causes, but my team had other plans. Massimo Pacetti, the Liberal member of Parliament and vice chair of the House finance committee, once asked me, "Is your office going to be useful or useless?" It was an important question and an important challenge. It targeted my own personal integrity and the mission of the PBO.

I learned only after I had left the PBO that two colleagues had made a pact when the speakers' letter arrived. It had been a tough day; we didn't know if we could survive the intense scrutiny, and our future was uncertain to say the least. But even at this lowest juncture, Ram and Sahir quietly declared to each other that the department would last at least one day longer than the man who had directed that letter our way, the parliamentary librarian, Bill Young. As it turned out, they were both still standing as members of the PBO when they attended Young's retirement party in December of 2011. It was a minor victory, I suppose, but a victory nonetheless.

SIX
MELTDOWN

Financial failures on Wall Street started piling up in September. Growth was slowing in Canada during the summer and early fall, though not totally flatlining just yet. In November, we released our first report on the economic and fiscal outlook for the country. Remember, we were still looking at numbers from the previous quarter, so although the sands were shifting beneath our feet, the available data did not yet reflect that reality. During the early part of November, Mostafa and I attended a conference in Chicago put on by Global Insight, an international economic forecasting firm. What we heard at that conference confirmed what we had been seeing the previous two months. Using the macro forecasting model designed by Global Insight, our analysts had produced a "Made in Canada" fiscal forecast. The people involved in this project were not those who had worked on the Afghanistan report. A relatively small group of very experienced colleagues, including Mostafa and Chris Matier, dove into the work. Both men had once headed forecasting at the finance department, so they knew their stuff.

As we examined available data, we determined several important potential outcomes. Based on our research, there appeared to be nothing but black clouds on the economic horizon. We believed that this would be a worldwide event, not an isolated or regional occurrence; everyone was going to pay a price in some way, shape, or form. Canada, though only a small player in the world economy, would nevertheless be affected as well. To make matters worse, economic forecasts from some key sources kept changing very quickly, which is always a negative indicator since it says that knowledgeable people can't get their heads around the data points. Once we put it all together, there was only one possible conclusion based on our modelling. We finished our report and got ready to go public.

Parliament was not yet in session after the recent election, so we held a briefing in a room at the Centre Block, again causing a stir on the Hill by providing numbers and analysis to Parliament and Canadians not yet provided by the government. The event garnered some significant media coverage, and we briefed MPs and the media at that gathering. Thomas Mulcair of the NDP was there, as was John McCallum of the Liberals; both were their respective parties' finance critics at the time. The event was very well attended and it clearly demonstrated to our team that the Afghanistan report had garnered us some traction. Everyone involved in the production of that report sat together as details were shared and clarified. We noted that there was a great likelihood of a pending recession and fiscal deficits within the country starting in 2009, but we had no idea at the time what kind of stir that report would create. I ended up doing interviews with respected journalists such as Don Newman and Craig Oliver to explain what we had produced and why we felt the country was on the verge of a recession. That particular briefing truly helped to cement a solid working relationship with members of the media, and our openness with the press probably saved us initially and helped liberate the PBO over time. Support from the media meant any effort by the government to impede the work of the

PBO would have a political cost. I remember vividly an exchange between some of our people and the Global News anchor, Kevin Newman. It was Sahir who asked, "Why are you people in the press willing to help us?" Newman answered, "Because we're both in the same business." Sahir then asked, "And what business would that be?" to which Newman smiled and said, "The transparency business." I've never forgotten those words.

Of course, our report and the means by which we openly announced and distributed its contents were not well received by many in the Conservative minority government, and I can understand why. For the previous eleven consecutive years, the government of the day had been running with a surplus; now, we were predicting a recession on the horizon. Our forecasting was simply not good public relations for those in charge of the public purse at the time. In hindsight, at that early stage, the PBO didn't have any kind of proven track record yet. We were still in our infancy, with less than one year on the job. And even if we had had a track record, no one is clairvoyant when it comes to the economy and the future, particularly when it comes to turning points. It's like trying to call the high or low point of a particular stock on the TSE—very difficult to do. You can pick ranges of results but to be spot on every time is virtually impossible. Any economist who says with one hundred percent certainty that something is going to happen in the future should not be trusted. No one can predict exactly what will transpire in the financial future of a country, so the government had every right to call us out on our predictions. Economists are not psychics. But we had confidence in our methodologies and judgment. We knew we were in the ballpark. As history shows, our forecasts would be counter to those provided by the government only a week later.

Why did we go public with our numbers ahead of the government? Were we trying to grandstand? The answer is that we provided our information before the government forecast was released because we didn't want to appear to be an agency that simply waited for the government to speak and then reacted to its pronouncements. Had we chosen to wait to release our numbers and then agreed with their estimates after they went public, we would have been perceived as just another mouthpiece for the government. On the other hand, if we disagreed after the fact with their predictions, we might be painted as some renegade appendage that was working in concert with the opposition parties. All of us genuinely felt that coming out with our estimates ahead of the government would be doing them a favour. I even called one of the senior officials at finance to let him know what we would be stating in our findings in advance of the event. I felt that it would give them a chance to reposition their analysis and communications. But the opposite occurred. We were vilified for coming out ahead of the government and senior Conservatives attempted to make us look like we didn't know what we were doing. They still went ahead with their "all clear" report, and that would end up being problematic for the government. One of our slides during that presentation addressed the need for stimulus packages in such a dire economic climate. The slide said something like: "Stimulus—Timely/Temporary/Targeted." History would prove our assertions to be close to the mark.

Finance minister Flaherty's report a week later was not at all what I had imagined it would be, nor did its contents match our findings in the least. He maintained that there was no recession, and no deficit for Canada in the year ahead. Unfortunately for the government, within days of its report, one of the most devastating economic catastrophes of the century would take hold, not only in Canada but around the world. I think that government officials responsible for the faulty forecast got caught with their pants down in no small measure because of "small group thinking." There was always a very tight inner circle for that government, which is probably how Prime Minister Harper liked to operate. The problem with that kind of organization is that when things go bad, they can go bad in a hurry. Running a closed shop has its advantages, but it has its disadvantages as well, and the government found that out the hard way. Everyone in Canada, from the financial community to average citizens, could plainly see that a recession was underway. It would be an economic perfect storm in the United States, the likes of which had not been seen since the Great Depression of the 1930s. And of course, in economic terms, we are joined at the hip with our friends south of the border.

Minister of Finance James Flaherty's viewpoint had obviously been skewed at least, or biased and incompetent at worst. That reality caused a furor on Parliament Hill as opposition leaders called into question the ability of the government to lead, given that it had missed the mark so badly on its economic forecast. They claimed that Canadians no longer had any confidence in the government and explicitly mentioned the PBO forecast. They had a point. It was an issue wholly brought on by Prime Minister Harper and Minister of Finance Flaherty because of their erroneous economic forecast. That mistake created two new realities. First, the government's ability to lead would come under greater scrutiny by the media. And second, the fact that our forecast had been closer to the mark than that of the government gave us credibility in the eyes of the opposition, the media, and the public.

I also learned a couple of practical lessons. One was that the media's understanding of such issues is quite variable, which can lead to some interpretive problems. For instance, some members of the media often seek out an executive summary version of a report with key ideas listed. But our intent was to educate and assist them in digesting the meat that was attached to the bones of the data. Of course, that doesn't always happen. Deadlines are deadlines. Sometimes people are in a hurry and facts can get in the way of a good story, and that you simply cannot control. The other lesson was that people would often make the message their own. That is, they might twist the commentary and make assumptions at times that we might or might not agree with as the writers of that report. But that is the real world and that is how information can be used by anyone, so you accept it as fact when you release your materials. If it gets twisted, so be it. We were accountable for what we reported, while others would be accountable for how they interpreted our information. It is one of the reasons we often tried to explain in great detail how we arrived at final numbers, regardless of the project. We wanted that information to be understood by all concerned stakeholders.

The media learned some things as well. After that report went public, certain newspeople such as CBC TV host Don Newman started to understand that the PBO was actually accessible and prepared to provide viable and reliable information for their consumption. I can remember doing one interview with Newman in which he introduced my segment by saying, "And now we have an interview with the *independent* PBO, Kevin Page," with emphasis on that word *independent*. The media played it up because they wanted us independent—it was good business for them as well as the country at large. The fact that most ministers of the government had gone missing in action for the press in recent times only served to heighten our appeal. The fact was that our data was meaningful. The fact was that the government seemed to be circling their wagons and avoiding the media where possible. Those factors undoubtedly worked in our favour.

At the end of 2008, the opposition parties started to publicly discuss the option of forming a coalition government in light of the Conservatives' faulty economic forecast. At one point, all of the opposition leaders held a press briefing that mentioned the work of the PBO and how it was more accurate than the government's estimates. Opposition leaders were using our data as the basis for *their* planning. The game of politics was about to be played out in a big way. But we could never have dreamed that our first fiscal forecast would end up playing as big a role in the political history of our country as it did. We could never have imagined that our claims of an impending economic downturn would play a part in the eventual proroguing of Canada's Parliament. But that is exactly what happened.

For all of us at the Parliamentary Budget Office, the first year of our existence had been historic in many ways and a trying time to say the least. But the overwhelmingly positive commentary about the Afghanistan war costing and fiscal forecast strengthened our resolve as a group. We knew that we could get the job done. We knew that the media could provide a platform for our transparent approach to reporting our findings. Though still in its infancy, the PBO had already taken form as a lean, mean, efficient machine that was getting increasing attention on Parliament Hill and across the entire country.

Still, we hung on for dear life.

SEVEN
ATTEMPTING TO HOGTIE THE PBO

The Parliamentary Budget Office had not received a great deal of cooperation from the Harper government during the start-up phase of its existence. In our second year, 2009, things got worse.

The federal election in October 2008 had produced another Conservative minority government with Prime Minister Harper at the helm. But the opposition leaders began making serious public noise after finance minister Flaherty's fall economic statement. They were not impressed as, frankly, the finance minister had completely missed the mark on the economic trends for 2009. Those same opposition leaders took to the airwaves and raised the spectre of a government that had lost the confidence of Parliament. Their argument was that the finance minister's announcement had been ill conceived, from an economic perspective as well as from a policy standpoint. Flaherty's competence was questioned and there was a lot of sabre-rattling. Prime Minister Harper, sensing the collapse of his government, went to the governor general and requested a proroguing of Parliament so as to reconstitute a budget that would be more acceptable to the country. Shortly thereafter, on December 4, 2008, Governor

General Michaëlle Jean granted the prime minister his wish, and Parliament was prorogued.

Such occurrences are relatively rare and I wonder how many people at the time in Ottawa (or anywhere else in Canada for that matter) were thinking, "I didn't see that one coming." I know that I was one of them. But it was a crafty political strategy on the part of the prime minister, one that bought him and the government much-needed time to regroup. The plan was for Parliament to be reconvened on January 26, 2009, with a budget to be delivered the following day. The Liberal Party would eventually support that new budget, enabling the Conservatives to continue leading with their minority. The budget of 2009 would reflect many of the predictions that we had put forward in our fiscal forecast in the fall. We had projected that the economy was headed for a deep recession. It was. We had stated that a federal deficit would return. It did. Economic uncertainty prevailed and consumer confidence declined. As a result of these unusually difficult economic circumstances, the need for some type of stimulus program was obvious.

The economic landscape had changed dramatically in less than the year in which the PBO had been in existence. I don't believe anyone could have envisioned the degree to which the recession would grab hold of economies around the world. It started in 2008 with the collapse on Wall Street and the U.S. sub-prime mortgage scandal, and worsened as 2009 unfolded. The financial tectonic plates were crumbling and Canada had no immunity from these economic forces. Journalists and pundits were attempting to assess how the government was responding as the economic catastrophe was being played out. Obviously, given Flaherty's optimistic proclamations during October 2008, the government was probably not prepared for what was happening on the world economic stage. Flaherty had incorrectly surmised that there was no imminent economic downturn. At the PBO we had disagreed with the finance minister's assumptions and were subsequently proven correct. With that reality, we felt that it was necessary to get involved with a 2009 budget assessment. We wanted to perform a macro analysis using tools not readily provided by the government in order to measure such areas as output gaps (Where was the economy relative to its potential?); cyclically adjusted budget balances (How much of the new deficits would be cyclical or structural in nature?); and long-term sustainability (Did we have a fiscal structure in place that could stabilize debt relative to gross domestic product [GDP] in the face of aging demographics?). That's a lot of fancy economist talk for "We wanted to see how things were shaping up for average Canadians in the big picture—now and into the future." Before any government begins making important decisions on the size of a stimulus package, it needs to utilize the proper tools to identify what is actually required. You can't always be totally confident that any given plan will work, but if you use the proper tools in forecasting and economic analysis, your chances for success are much better.

At the same time, the PBO was continuing to write and research on a broad range of timely issues. One of our more significant endeavours was related to the funding of Aboriginal education and again, it would put us in conflict with the government. We were approached by the NDP member of Parliament for Timmins, Ontario, Charles Angus, who was asking why his riding was not going to receive a new school for Aboriginal children. He wanted detailed information in order to better understand the process inherent in such decisions and we thought that it was a valid request. We decided that we would look at how the Department of Indian Affairs and Northern Development (now known as Aboriginal Affairs and Northern

Development Canada) determined funding. We found that there was no model to follow. It appeared that the people in charge of distributing funding were simply throwing darts at an imaginary target. It made no sense. Their protocols looked like a patchwork to us, with a lot of guesswork at play. So Ram Mathilakath and Ash Rajekar went about the task of building a model.

Ram and Ash wanted to establish a fiscal approach that would ensure adequate educational funding now and into the future for Aboriginal communities. They began with questions: Why are Aboriginal children apparently not enjoying the same type of financial support that other Canadian kids are? What assets are already in place? What do we need to set aside in order to maintain those assets? What are possible replacement costs for those assets once they are no longer viable or sustainable? It was a straightforward capital budgeting approach used by school boards across the country, yet it was not used by the federal government for Aboriginal children.

Our report released in May 2009 showed that there was an annual shortfall of $100 million to $200 million for educational funding in Aboriginal communities. It also suggested the need for a more transparent targeting mechanism. The report elicited a strong response from the government, as expected, claiming that we were way off base. This particular assertion irked Ash and Ram to no end because they had used the government's own data to arrive at their conclusions.

One evening shortly after our Aboriginal report release, Pat Brown informed me that former prime minister Paul Martin was on the phone with a request: "Can you provide me with a brief on the Aboriginal report?" Aboriginal conditions and rights have been a personal crusade for Martin and he wanted as much current and meaningful information as he could muster. He also congratulated the PBO on garnering a lot of credibility in such a short time, but added, "I probably wouldn't have wanted you looking over my shoulder when I was finance minister." We would receive words of encouragement from other distinguished Canadians as well, such as former prime minister Joe Clark and the great Aboriginal leader Phil Fontaine. Stars shine the brightest when it's darkest outside.

Eventually, in part as a result of our having highlighted the issue, Aboriginal funding for the next fiscal year was increased through the government's economic action plan to provide stimulus funding. Many years later, the government would recognize the broader extent of this funding shortfall—a funding gap that was allowed to build over many years—but I continue to argue that the funding formula itself, even to this day, remains flawed.

More trouble was brewing. On May 14, 2009, an event occurred that had the potential to derail the most important operations of the PBO. I was asked to attend a meeting of the Standing Joint Committee for the Library of Parliament, and I knew from the outset what was going to take place. Our reporting on Canadian involvement in Afghanistan in the fall of 2008 had rubbed some politicians the wrong way. Our prediction of an economic downturn had contradicted the federal government's forecast and had ruffled some feathers as well. I had been accused by some members of Parliament of straying outside my boundaries as the PBO. Clearly, somebody thought that I had been showing too many teeth, and as a result, this committee had been struck as a means of "de-fanging" any future impact of the PBO. It had been tasked to review the operations of my office and my actions, in keeping with the issues highlighted by the two speakers in the October 2008 letter. In my estimation, it was nothing more than a politically inspired kangaroo court, and it was almost inevitable that it would turn into an acrimonious affair. It did. The entire meeting became a political back and forth that, in large measure, missed the essence of what role the PBO could play within our government. I regarded it as an attempt to undermine and muzzle us. This public attempt to hogtie our operation, if accomplished, would severely restrict our ability to provide important information for parliamentarians as a means to hold the government to account. More specifically, they needed to hold the *executive branch* to account. As the committee proceedings unfolded, a lineup of former parliamentarians had been assembled as witnesses and brought in to testify that I should be held in contempt of Parliament for my actions as the PBO. It became very personal. Intimidation and fearmongering were all too common tactics of the Harper government. They were a mean-spirited bunch and I've never understood the need for that kind of approach. But perhaps even more frightening than the intimidation tactics themselves is the fact that, in large measure, those tactics worked. If you displeased the people at the top, you were open to ridicule or even dismissal. It made for a closed-shop atmosphere that I can only surmise was a part of their strategy to keep power. The PBO increasingly came under fire from the federal government, often in the form of these personal attacks. It seemed as if the people in charge had determined very early in my mandate that I was to be undermined whenever possible and however possible. They tried to challenge the supposed boundaries of the PBO. I argued that those boundaries were not legislated, were extremely confusing, and in many cases represented revisionist history in their proposed application. They countered by trying to marginalize who we were and what we were attempting to do.

I began hearing from sympathetic senior civil servants, friends, and colleagues of mine in Ottawa, who said that I should watch my step, and I was told on more than one occasion that government officials had apparently been investigating my background. If the government had been able to collect information that might have linked me to a pack of stolen gum from a drug store when I was eleven years old, I'm sure the information would have been leaked! Regardless of this climate, we kept plugging along. Any attempt at intimidation on their part simply wouldn't work because they didn't understand what was happening back at the office. Had they managed to bring me down personally, they still would have had to deal with the rest of the PBO team. Attempting to strong-arm me only served to inflame an already upset group at the office, and the PBO backbone just kept growing stronger.

But they attacked nevertheless and it led to some interesting theatre on May 14. There were some heated exchanges between me and Conservative senator Terry Stratton (Manitoba), Liberal MPs Mauril Bélanger (Ottawa–Vanier) and Ken Dryden (York Centre), and others, primarily about the independence of the work of the PBO. Their contention was that if any MP made a request to our office for costing information, then that information should stay private or in confidence with the member of Parliament who requested the information. We fundamentally disagreed, advocating instead for openness and transparency of information for all citizens. There was some tough commentary from across the table, combined with many cold stares aimed in my direction. They insinuated that I was showboating. I responded by asking that they simply *hold me accountable for the work*. I had to handle questions pertaining to the operating model of the PBO from some people in the room who were obviously "measuring those drapes" again, which meant that parts of the commentary and criticism were designed for effect and career enhancement while having very little to do with reality. It's important to keep calm and focused when the cannons are being pointed at your head, but of course, that is easier said than done. Yet I did feel relatively comfortable and calm in that setting, perhaps because I knew we were on solid ground. Specifically, I had faith in the quality of work that we were producing and that the work could stand on its own. As the meeting moved on, I watched a succession of people speak for their allotted five minutes. Much of the content was of a negative nature, a designed course to show where the PBO had gone astray. But, at some junctures, particular individuals brought clarity and fairness to the proceedings, none more eloquently than the man serving as the finance critic for the New Democratic Party at the time, Thomas Mulcair. He demanded that our original budget of $2.8 million be reinstituted so that the PBO could fulfill its mandate. And as to that mandate, Mulcair stated: "There is an old rule in legislation that when writing a statute, it is not sufficient to be clear enough so a person in good faith can understand; it has to be clear enough so a person in bad faith cannot *misunderstand*. I think we are in that second category now. We do not need to change the statute if we return to the first category." Well said! But I knew when I left that meeting that we were in for some rough waters.

Eventually, on June 16, 2009, the Joint Committee issued a report that they wanted to include ten recommendations specific to the PBO. My feeling was and remains that the fix was in right from the first moment the committee had been struck. The issue of transparency was at stake. One of their ten recommendations stated that the data from our reports should remain confidential, whereas we called for everything to be posted to the website. This was very important turf for us to defend and represented the very foundation upon which our office had been created. If we were forced to withhold information from the public, the credibility of the PBO would take a tremendous hit. Other recommendations dealt with a range of issues including working relationships in the Library of Parliament and the potential return of the PBO budget to its original level. But the key issues for us were the ownership of the analysis and the release of all PBO reports.

Initially, the signs were not very positive. Within days, the Joint Committee report received concurrence in the Senate, which was the first potential nail in the PBO coffin. If the House of Commons approved the committee's recommendations as well, we would be dead and buried. If that happened, I knew that there could only be one outcome for me, as the concept of transparency through publishing to our website was one of those principles that I was prepared to resign over. Looking back, I had watched with great respect and empathy when my former boss, Munir Sheikh, had done exactly that to protest the removal of the mandatory component of the long-form census. But I had never dreamed that someday I might find myself in the same position.

Then things took a turn for the better. First, on a personal level, I began receiving messages from several MPs and other notables on the Hill who asked me to stay on regardless of the House vote on the recommendations. Mulcair was one of the first to call. He was convinced that I should stay on and "fight the good fight." He wanted me and my office to pursue our advocacy for an independent PBO, one where the transparency issue was understood and guaranteed, and I should stay and build that office over my five-year term. Our conversation lifted my spirits immeasurably. Shortly thereafter, NDP leader Jack Layton called to ask how I was holding up. He asked my views on how the entire office was evolving and encouraged me to stay on as the parliamentary budget officer as well. I'm not a rookie on Parliament Hill, so I understand that politics may be associated with such communications. However, Layton seemed truly genuine in his comments.

I rode my bike home that day from work, and during the twenty-five-kilometre journey, I kept coming back to that conversation. I had told Layton I was thinking about quitting. To that, he said, "No way. You cannot quit. The work of your group is too important. If you need more support from parliamentarians, we can help." In addition to those calls of encouragement, a group of one hundred economists signed on to social media to support the work of the PBO, an extraordinary measure that buoyed everyone at the office. And then, as always, there was my wife Julie. Through all the difficult times she delivered a very simple and consistent message for me: "You can't quit." Day after day, she gave me strength to carry on.

Mostafa and Sahir both suggested that we should just ignore the ten recommendations and treat them as what they were—a political gesture having nothing to do with our mandate. They advised that we should all just keep putting our research up on the website and keep doing reports. And that is exactly what we did. We could only hope that maybe the committee members would have short memories or perhaps the political landscape would shift and the PBO would become yesterday's news. If we could just survive in the short term, we believed, the long term would take care of itself.

In August, I drafted an action plan in response to the committee's ten recommendations in which I detailed our commitment to continue publicly reporting our findings. I sent the report to all members of the committee, stating why the PBO could not survive in a meaningful way if we were forced to keep our findings confidential. Further, I proposed that we would establish specific terms of reference for all work projects. This I considered a strategic tool we could implement in order to work around the committee recommendation that all PBO reports would have to be confidential until released by the member of Parliament who had requested the report. I included an assessment of analytical approaches to costing questions, information and analytical requirements, access to expertise, timelines, and release strategies. It demonstrated that we needed to reach out to experts in order to ensure accuracy. Therefore, maintaining confidentiality would not work—quite the opposite: it would hinder the quality of the research. We believed that our office should not be asked to labour on a project for months, using taxpayers' money, only to find out that the benefit of the work would not be made public because an MP did not like the analysis provided. Inevitably, the accountability would rest squarely on my shoulders as the person leading the office.

My action plan was not well received. The committee chair, Liberal senator Sharon Carstairs, and parliamentary librarian Bill Young were not pleased that I had sent copies to all committee members. Senator Carstairs' initial response to me was simply that she was very disappointed. But she let me know in no uncertain terms during follow-up phone calls that she did not approve of either the content or the protocol I used to release the information. In the days just after I sent that document, I also met privately with Bill Young, and the look on his face said it all: he knew that by making the action plan available to all committee members, we had regained the upper hand in the matter of releasing documents. But the game was far from over. It was a time of great tension.

Globe and Mail political columnist John Ibbitson asked to see a copy of my action plan, the response to the ten Joint Standing Committee recommendations, and I happily obliged. I saw no reason not to share it with him as we were supposed to be operating with transparency; I had not written that document so that it could be kept secret. John recognized the report for what it was—an "up yours" proclamation, if I may paraphrase and dilute John's remarks. We knew that we needed help on this and John Ibbitson was someone who could get the message out in a hurry. It was the notion of transparency working at its best—at least from our perspective at the Parliamentary Budget Office.

One more important event occurred that involved Sahir and a member of the political machinery for the Liberal Party of Canada. The Senate vote on the Joint Committee recommendations had not gone our way. If a second vote was taken, this time in the House of Commons, and if the Liberals voted with the Conservatives, then the PBO as we knew it would be changed forever. Frankly, that was what appeared to be in the cards. However, in the days leading up to the vote, quite by accident, Sahir met an important Liberal staff member on the street outside our offices. The two engaged in a discussion about the importance of the PBO and the pending vote, and Sahir finally asked him, "Have the Liberals totally forgotten about the sponsorship scandal already?" It was a political point—the idea that even after having been turfed from power, the Liberals had not learned the lesson that without transparency, power can indeed become corrupt. Sahir's comment also implied that the Liberals were prepared to side with the Conservatives in order to complete the de-fanging of our office. Had nothing changed in Ottawa? But at the same time, if a Sponsorgate could happen to the Liberals, perhaps the Conservatives could misstep as well. In that scenario, the Liberals would want an office such as ours bringing truth to light. I'll never know if that question stirred the conscience of that Liberal, but history shows that the House vote was never even taken. Basically, the Liberals shut it all down. Perhaps it was a purely political decision. Perhaps the Liberals genuinely felt that the PBO was good for the country. I just don't know. But whatever the rationale, it meant that those ten recommendations did not have full parliamentary support. We had new life. A tremendous load was lifted from our collective shoulders. We had won a reprieve.

In the fall of 2009, the PBO estimated that some of the fiscal deficit would be cyclical in nature but some was obviously structural. Policy makers didn't really need to worry very much about the cyclical part of deficits because that usually disappears once the economy recovers. But the structural part of the deficit was another issue. A structural deficit means that you're swimming with an economic rock tied around your neck over an extended period of time; in such circumstances, you have a good chance of sinking to the bottom of the lake. It's simplistic, I agree, but you get the point. We have seen some of the devastating outcomes of deepening structural deficits in countries such as Spain, Greece, and Italy in recent times. The PBO commented on the structural nature of our national deficit and noted that the government had created it in part by cutting sales and income taxes. The government reacted negatively to those assertions yet could provide no counteranalysis, a response that occurred over and over again and always dumbfounded me as an economist. If you have an argument, present it and let the chips fall where they may. But government officials always seemed to forget the part about presenting the argument.

In January 2010, Finance Minister Flaherty had stated that Canada did not have a structural deficit. To me, it seemed he didn't want to admit it because his government had inherited a structural surplus, not a deficit, and that would not play out well in the media. After tax cuts and spending increases, the surplus had disappeared and a modest structural deficit had been created. Finance officials did not release estimates until years later, which indicated that we did indeed have a structural deficit. We pushed to get people at finance to publish their estimates, hearing later from insiders that the minister was not happy his officials did publish the numbers. In the years ahead, specifically within Budget 2012, the government would launch an austerity program to get rid of that same structural deficit. They had known all along that there was a structural component to the deficit; they did not admit it, but their budget austerity policy betrayed that reality. They said otherwise publicly, but in truth took action to get rid of that structural deficit even though the economy remained weakened as it recovered from the recession in 2008–09.

On another front, in May 2009, a new Liberal leader replaced Stéphane Dion as the head of the official opposition party. Michael Ignatieff publicly supported the PBO, and due in part to his efforts, our budget was returned to its previously announced levels. That meant that we didn't have to reduce the size of the office and our work could continue. I liked Michael Ignatieff personally while respecting his understanding of the issues of the day. One night, just before we were going to release one of our major papers, he called simply to wish us well because he knew that the government was going to hit back at us. At the end of my tenure as PBO he sent me an email in which he thanked me for my service to the country. There was no political gain for him in sending that message—it was simply a gesture of kindness by the leader of the Liberals. Unfortunately for him as a leader, he was never able to mobilize the country—or his party, for that matter. The Liberals had a very weak agenda at that time, and as a party they were not very supportive of their leader. As well, the Conservatives did a substantial hatchet job on the man, portraying him as a Harvard snob, an elitist intellectual who came back to Canada only for personal glory.

After our report on funding of Aboriginal education, we produced one more major study in our second year. In it we investigated the long-term sustainability of the federal government's fiscal plan. It was a big job and one that caused a lot of internal debate within the office. I was uneasy about it, given the tumultuous state of the world's economy. But it was Mostafa who, in his typically controlled way, insisted that we *had* to undertake this project. He argued that this type of work was exactly where the PBO could be a positive influence, since politicians rarely tend to focus on the long term as doing so could be harmful to their political future. The major changes in the demographics of the Canadian population meant that such a study was important if we were to plan realistically. It would be a seventy-five-year projection with a fairly basic question at its centre: Do we as a nation have a fiscal structure in place that will stabilize debt relative to GDP in the long term? At the time, banks were stress testing their balance sheets. We wanted to do the same thing with our government's balance sheets. In essence, we were stress testing against an aging population.

What does all of that mean in real terms? How can Canadians make sense of a bunch of numbers and jumbled talk by economists? Here is one way to think about it: Would the funding currently in place take care of our aging population should someone develop, for example, a debilitating health issue such as Alzheimer's? To make it more personal, could the government with its current fiscal approach help if one of our own parents were diagnosed with dementia? Can we as a nation afford that kind of care *right now*? Will we afford it in thirty years should you or I develop Alzheimer's? And finally, in sixty or seventy years, what happens if one of our children develops some form of Alzheimer's—will the government be able to provide for their care? That hits home for me.

As we dug into the numbers, we found a fiscal gap between the total amount of needed government revenues and our spending that would need to be reduced so as to stabilize debt relative to GDP at current levels. The numbers didn't look very healthy for the future. We projected that the longer we waited to take action, the bigger that gap was going to become. Taking care of our aging population wouldn't be the only area that would be impacted if that gap wasn't filled quickly enough. When we reported our findings, not a single member of Parliament showed up for the briefing. I suppose it wasn't a very sexy topic to the average politician. Still, every media outlet sent representatives.

The second year of our tenure ended with what felt like a vindication. When the new budget was introduced early in 2009, all of us in the PBO noticed some striking features about what the government was suddenly proposing. The numbers they produced told us that on all major counts the government was now agreeing with our first fiscal forecast, the one we had released in November 2008 before the prorogation of Parliament. They might not have admitted it publicly, but for an economist the proof was in the numbers. We knew that we had been on point the whole time, and what's more, *we knew that the government now knew it as well.* That was very gratifying for our staff. A journalist once asked me if we were better forecasters than the government. The truth is that in any such estimate you use the best tools available to you, fuelled by the best research and data you can get your hands on, and then you simply release your report.

We had survived through our second year on the Hill. Political leaders changed and the economy continued to slide. We did as the speakers had advised early on in my time as PBO—we kept our collective heads down and kept on working. Appearing before the Joint Committee to defend the work and mandate of the PBO had taken a lot out of me personally but, by the end of 2009, I was off the mat. Our office had produced approximately twenty reports, averaging better than one per month since our creation in April 2008.

It was starting to look like the PBO just might be hanging around after all. But I must confess that as the year ended, I was still holding my breath.

EIGHT
PEOPLE, POLITICS, AND PROCESS

My relationship with several key people in the Harper government was—"interesting." But when I took the job as Canada's first parliamentary budget officer, I never envisioned the PBO as being involved in an "us versus them" dynamic. We were in our office to serve parliamentarians who had reasonable requests for costing or other fiscal information. But the relationship that had developed between our office and the ruling Conservative Party was, to put it mildly, somewhat strained. And as was their pattern, members of the governing party often made things personal, but from my perspective, those personal attacks only served to bolster the confidence of the team at the PBO. Why? Because the government rarely had anything negative to say about the *work* we produced. They might take cheap shots at me, but as time passed they learned to keep quiet about the content of the reports themselves—because the content was always solid and based on reliable data. We knew that key people in the government had a grudging respect for what we were producing and that kept the fires stoked at our office. But in the end, it wasn't our work that primarily upset the leaders of the government; rather, it was apparently the public face of the PBO that made their blood boil.

For the most part, the personal attacks were launched against me. Prime Minister Harper, Finance Minister Flaherty, and other cabinet ministers did not single out other individuals from our office. They wanted to divert attention whenever government projections didn't match those of the PBO and they had a focused target. But realistically, in those five years that I was in the PBO, the government and senior public service personnel never came back to Parliament or us with a substantive response on any of our reports. They didn't do it on Afghanistan, or on the F-35, the crime bill costing, or fiscal sustainability. Prime Minister Harper and his people simply wanted to create their own information boxes. They continually attempted to give the impression to Canadians through their communiqués and the media that they were expressing the views of a broad base across the country. Of course, much of that was nonsense—rhetoric and spin. But I have to admit that they really could sell. From my desk, I witnessed a consistent pattern wherein the government rarely seemed to provide significant or believable information as a comeback to our reports. Rather, they always shot back with the same tired accusations that the work emanating from our office was somehow partisan in nature or an academic exercise. Again, this was all a part of the deflection from reality, another attempt at making personal commentary the norm.

Inevitably, the government's particular approach, playing its cards tight to its vest, actually assisted the PBO in doing its job. Members of the media and MPs as well came to view us as one of the few vehicles through which they could find any relevant, meaningful information. Ours was a fundamentally different approach when it came to the dissemination of information. Media people were blown away by the fact that we were actually prepared to share data. Our model of operation was foreign to them, especially given the consistent stonewalling that they had been experiencing from the government. For instance, we offered them the chance to speak directly with our analysts on a given report before ever speaking with me. In that way they would have more information with which to ask me the right questions—the hard questions. The media soon came to realize that we had no fear, were hiding nothing, and were prepared to go on the record. Compared to what they were experiencing with the government and the public service in general, it was a relief for them. As a result, the prime minister's closed-shop environment began to work against him. He may not have enjoyed the profile we received, but the truth is that he helped create that profile. And he might not have appreciated our methods, but we served an increasingly useful purpose given the consistent lack of information provided by his government.

Of all the interactions I had with the Harper government, the most public and acrimonious undeniably occurred with Harper's minister of finance—Jim Flaherty. Nowhere was the ongoing strain more evident than in our dealings with finance. To be fair, it must be said that Jim Flaherty was under the gun as Canada's finance minister. He was running his ministry during a brutal economic blitzkrieg, a monetary unravelling the extent of which few saw coming. He was at the helm of finance, and it was an extremely difficult portfolio in a period when many fiscal outcomes were far beyond his control as he did not have the kind of freedom or latitude that previous finance ministers had enjoyed. The other principal factor that tied his hands was the fact that the prime minister in office and the clerk of the PCO both wanted to build budgets from the bottom up—effectively, to do the work of the finance department. It all meant that there wasn't much wiggle room for the finance minister. I have been told by many people who called Jim Flaherty a friend that he was a good, principled man. Unfortunately, I never got to know him personally. (His death only three weeks after announcing his retirement in 2014 meant that I would never have the chance to know him as a person separate from the political figure I often sparred with during occasional disagreements.) Once I became the PBO I had attempted to meet with him at various times during his tenure as finance minister, but we never seemed able to have that meeting for one reason or another. Some Conservative members told me that it would probably be better to meet with someone like Stockwell Day, then the president of the Treasury Board. They said that Day was pretty calm in most situations whereas Jim Flaherty often got pretty emotional, living up to his reputation as an "Irish Lion."

That whole situation between the minister of finance and our office was unfortunate and unnecessary. We were trying to build a solid legislative budget office for Canada, yet the Conservatives worked diligently to discredit the PBO virtually from the beginning of its existence. One can only speculate as to why they chose that course of action. They may have perceived us as a genuine threat to their political agenda. Perhaps they wanted to muzzle an organization such as ours that might make them look like poor fiscal forecasters and managers. But, in part as a result of the tenuous relationship we had with the minister of finance, our survival was constantly being debated through various media outlets and the public service network itself. That did not go unnoticed by members of my senior executive group. We decided to try to clear the air and so, early in 2010, we asked for and received a face-to-face meeting with Finance Minister Flaherty at his office on Parliament Hill.

Sahir, Mostafa, and Ram were in the room with me as we sat down with Jim Flaherty. The minister of justice, Vic Toews, was also present, as were the finance minister's assistants. I don't know why Toews was asked to attend that particular meeting, as he had virtually nothing to do with what we were about to discuss. Perhaps he was just another shield—someone to even out the numbers in the room. Mind you, we had been out front on some justice issues, including the proposed crime bill, so perhaps he felt a need to hear from our camp. I do not remember a thing that Toews said, but we weren't there for chit-chat with the justice minister. We were there to see one man and one man only—Jim Flaherty. As things got underway I remember being physically very close to the finance minister, seated just across from him at a small table. He looked friendly enough, I thought. He did a lot of listening and remained very quiet throughout most of the proceedings. I remember thinking to myself that we were being assessed by the man, and that was okay—we were assessing him as well. This was a chance to forge something positive.

Aside from some general comments during the introductions that day, he only interjected on one occasion the entire time we were in his office: he wanted to know why the PBO relationship with the federal government had become so adversarial. I looked him in the eye and explained that we didn't want an adversarial relationship. Rather, we were simply attempting to do our job as outlined in the act of Parliament that his government had been instrumental in creating. I said that we were doing the best independent financial analysis we could. He listened very carefully to my response and appeared to give my comments great thought. It was hardly antagonistic on either side. This was no showdown; there were no threats, no accusations, and no table-pounding with clenched fists. To this day I am convinced that Flaherty believed that we were doing our jobs, even though he must have felt politically compelled to publicly argue otherwise. And I further believe that the minister knew full well that we were not exceeding our mandate, because he would have undoubtedly been briefed by people whom many of us at

the PBO knew well and had worked with over the years. My
sense is that Flaherty must have been told in private that our
work at the PBO was solid and nonpartisan, and so I'll never
really know why he apparently chose to disregard such information. After our meeting, Flaherty told the media that we had
discussed parameters of our relationship. But the reality is that we
only had one meeting, and nothing of real substance ever came
of it. He would continue a consistent pattern of questioning our
credibility in the press over the next several years. He never let up.

Being attacked by the prime minister and his finance minister
was serious stuff, especially in the context of a minority government where confidence meant everything. It garnered a lot of
media attention to be sure, on issues like the F-35 or deficit
projections. But Stephen Harper and Jim Flaherty weren't the
only people on the Hill who presented a threat to the long-term
survival of the PBO. The parliamentary librarian, Bill Young,
might not have had the profile of the prime minister or his
finance minister, yet the problems that would crop up around
our involvement with the parliamentary library were no less
taxing on my time and energy. Bill Young was a career civil
servant who had served with dignity, and I understood that he
was simply executing his duties in his position as he saw fit.
During the first few years of PBO operations, I was still meeting
with Bill approximately every two weeks; at the same time, there
were also regular meetings with the senior management group
from the Library of Parliament. I never understood why we had
to have those meetings because, as they related to my role as
head of the PBO, they were a complete waste of time. The
country was burning under us as the recession worsened, yet
they wanted me to talk about the future of the library. No
disrespect is intended, but I couldn't have cared less what course
the library would end up taking because it had absolutely

nothing to do with our mandate at the PBO. Eventually I told Sahir and Mostafa that I would no longer sit in on those library meetings—I was done. But they both expressed their view that we should have eyes and ears at the table, so both volunteered to start attending in my place. Now that, my friends, is dedication and sacrifice of the highest order!

Besides, the criticism had begun to feel personal. At one point during a conversation, Bill made a reference to some of the people who worked with me at the PBO as my crew of "public service refugees." Perhaps it was an attempt at humour, but the so-called refugees—Sahir, Mostafa, Ram, and Tolga—weren't laughing when I shared that line. At the same time, we had picked up on some trash talk from the public service grapevine as well. But the truth is that the troubles with the finance minister, the tiff with the parliamentary librarian over the "refugee" comment, and the occasional barbs from within the ranks of the civil service only served to galvanize the office. Increasingly, an "us against the world" mentality took hold at the PBO.

As the gap widened between our analysis and the government's analysis of various expenditures, we began to be painted with a particular brush by the government, portrayed as a rogue group whose members were determined to undermine the government on behalf of the opposition. The constant public barrage by ministers such as Flaherty, Toews, and Day, in combination with persistent questioning about partisanship by many members of various governmental committees, was relentless. The truth is that I cannot recall even one conversation at the PBO that involved any one of us proposing to "get" Prime Minister Harper or anyone in his government on a particular issue. I have no doubt that key people within his caucus might have felt otherwise, but we tried to be as neutral in our assessments as possible, with unbiased data leading our reporting.

Our role was simply to get the best data we could, assess it in the best way we could, and then report what we found, regardless of the implications for any political party. There wasn't a PBO vendetta against the government. Perhaps no better example of that reality was in the report we delivered that year about the G8 and G20 summit security costs.

In 2010, Prime Minister Harper and his government came under some harsh criticism from opposition parties as well as the press when the high cost for security at the summit meetings was reported. But accusations went beyond security costs. The government was also taken to task for supposedly moving money around to pay for local legacy work associated with the summits. There were accusations that monies were being taken from other ridings and put into Muskoka in order to beautify it and leave a lasting impression. Industry Minister Tony Clement was accused of moving funds into his Muskoka riding that might have been designed to support, for example, border infrastructure.

We decided to undertake the task of analyzing the summit costs after the government had sent out its own projections for the events. Our analysis was finished and released approximately one month after the government had provided its own data. We concluded that in spite of what many critics might have believed, the federal government had actually been transparent in its estimates and actual spending on security for the G8 and G20 summits. The report gave the government high marks and suggested that planned costs for the G8 summit in Huntsville, Ontario, and G20 in Toronto were not out of line with previous summits held under the watch of a different government in Canada. We received a lot of meaningful assistance from senior public servants in securing information for this report, and that implied something else as well. Their compliance in this one area suggested to me that when it was in *their* best interests (as opposed to Parliament's), information would be forthcoming. What we found and reported should have signalled that we weren't out to get the government. Rather, we were out to get transparency, plain and simple.

We finally had some support from our own government agencies, but our American contacts also provided vital information about their experiences with a summit that had been held years earlier in Pittsburgh, Pennsylvania. They knew how to lock down a city—they understood all the costs. Our report shed a positive light on the Conservative government's handling of the summits and assisted in deflecting unfounded criticism.

All the while, the clock kept ticking on my time at the PBO. I understood from the beginning of my tenure that there would be a very definite endpoint to my stay in the position—it would come in at most five years if we could manage to survive, less if we had the rug somehow pulled from under us. We were determined to use well whatever time we had left, and so produced new reports while updating some of the data we had previously created. For instance, we reviewed and expanded our analysis on the long-term fiscal sustainability of the federal government that we had begun in 2009, and eventually proposed that there was also a fiscal gap at the provincial–territorial level. Finance Minister Flaherty went on the offensive, stating publicly that there was no federal fiscal gap. And at the time that was true—he just left out any mention of the fiscal circumstances at the provincial–territorial level. Down the road, when the government announced it would reduce the rate of growth of the Canada Health Transfer in late 2011, the PBO showed that while the gap at the federal level had been eliminated (at least on paper), the shortfall at the provincial–territorial level just got bigger as those jurisdictions will now bear more of the brunt of rising health care costs. It was a type of economic shell game designed to clean up the books for the feds while letting the provinces shoulder more and more responsibility.

Flaherty also noted at one point that our reporting on long-term government sustainability was basically academic in nature even though most other OECD countries were preparing this very same kind of work at the same time. Our report indicated that the federal government had a modest long-term fiscal gap—meaning that as a nation we did not have a fiscal structure in place that would stabilize debt relative to GDP in the face of aging demographics. We needed decisions on taxes and spending programs to make our fiscal situation sustainable. The government basically turned up its nose at the analysis. We went further and released a report that looked at gaps in quarterly reporting on budget and delays in the rollout of the Infrastructure Stimulus Fund, a two-year $4 billion cost-shared initiative with provinces and municipalities to fix existing infrastructure and build new assets. Whenever we asked for any assistance from the government, we were inevitably stonewalled. In this instance, the deputy minister of transport eventually did send us some information, but not in the form of electronic files. Rather, she provided us with boxes of paper that we would have to spend crucial manpower hours sorting out. This type of tactic was not the exception but rather the rule. Why? Because both the public service and various branches of the government chose to react negatively to our work. Of course, I knew many of those same people from my career in public service, so it was especially perplexing when I knew from private conversations with many of them that they actually agreed with our approach at the PBO. Those may have been their private assertions, but their public pronouncements became far more guarded. I wonder why.

One of the tenets of the Conservative regime was its "tough on crime" stance. The government sought to change the Criminal Code of Canada so as to introduce more punitive measures. The Truth in Sentencing Act (TSA) was intended to amend the Code to limit the credit a judge may allow for any time spent in pre-sentencing custody in order to reduce the punishment to be imposed at sentencing, commonly called "credit for time served." Under the new act, a judge may allow a credit of one day for each day spent in presentencing custody (instead of the typical two days allowed under the old act). However, if and only if the circumstances justify it, a judge may allow a maximum credit of one and one-half days for each day spent in presentencing custody. This was a major plank of the government's "tough on crime" agenda. It would also turn out to be the most expensive aspect of their platform. You don't have to be an economist to realize that if you keep people in jail longer and add to the numbers who are incarcerated, your costs will inevitably increase. Any government has the right to declare that it is going to be tough on crime as a part of its political agenda, but it should have to come clean on the actual costs of implementing such an agenda. In this case, no hard numbers were provided. The Conservatives were telling members of Parliament to study and vote as told, on demand, on a new bill that would change the Criminal Code of Canada without any financial basis for their vote. There was no White Paper explaining the policy change. There was no financial costing analysis. No information appeared in the federal budget or in the Correctional Service of Canada Report on Plans and Priorities. Nothing. All this from a government selling itself as a good fiscal manager—a government that brought in the Accountability Act to renew Parliament. It was hypocrisy at its highest level—with no financial analysis, no transparency, and no accountability. Canadians need to know this.

We decided to undertake this particular costing project based upon a request from Mark Holland, at that time the Liberal MP from Ajax–Pickering. The bill was already in second reading when we started the work, so time was short. As we got closer to releasing our report in the spring of 2010, news began circulating that the contents of our findings would highlight a significant fiscal cost for both the federal government and the provincial governments. Suddenly, the communications from Parliament Hill started to change. Justice Minister Toews indicated that his office was not releasing financial information because of difficulties in estimating costs due to uncertainty. Yet it is the very essence of governmental responsibility to make such forecasts. That responsibility weighs even more heavily in times of uncertainty, when people need information and direction. Eventually the minister conceded that the federal cost would be pegged at approximately $2 billion over a five-year period—in line with PBO estimates.

When we did release our report about the costs of the "tough on crime" legislation, it called into question the cost of proposed higher rates of incarceration at the federal and provincial levels. The government and public service were under pressure to release data about the costs of incarcerating higher numbers of inmates, but before our report, the government had refused to release any numbers, choosing instead to consistently cite "cabinet confidentiality" as a main reason for the secrecy. Our office provided the first framework to understand the overall cost of the Canadian criminal justice system. The work was required to better understand the long-term implications of numerous changes to the system, and the paper analyzed the growth of different sectors such as security and corrections. Our findings indicated that costs would increase significantly even as the overall crime rate was falling.

The report was prepared by Ram Mathilakath and Ash Rajekar with leadership and direction from Sahir Khan—the same team that had drafted our reports on the cost of the Afghanistan war and on rebuilding the Aboriginal educational infrastructure. They drew on the expertise of many people, from university professors to people working in the correctional system. It was not a traditional public sector way of doing work, as most of the public servants I knew were turning away from financial modelling for costing and appeared to have embraced a new normal of back-of-the-envelope types of calculations for PowerPoint presentations. There was little or no discussion of cost drivers, assumptions, various scenarios, or uncertainty—nothing that would stand up to scrutiny. In many cases, they were not allowed to talk to experts. They found themselves working for a government that did not seem to want to know the estimated cost of its own proposed programs. The government would simply send out a tagline such as "We want to be tough on crime" and that was it.

We decided to dig a little deeper and undertook two analyses. One was a backward-looking estimate that asked, "What would happen if a prisoner's change in remand—the loss of a day of credit for time served before sentencing—was in place in 2007–08?" We also built a forward-looking estimate model, a probabilistic simulation model (fancy term!) to capture the projected flow and costs of inmates moving into and out of our correctional services system. Both models and estimates were peer-reviewed. The forward-looking model was very sophisticated, and initially I was very concerned that we were overbuilding the model and pushed for a simpler approach and tests of reasonableness. Over a weekend, my colleague and friend Ash built a spreadsheet model that I felt would help with the communications. The basic point was the bottom line: incarceration is expensive.

A couple of key points provide a sense of the expense that accrues to the taxpaying public as a result of prisoner incarceration. For example, for the 2007–08 fiscal year, the funding per cell in operations and capital appropriation was about $145 000 per inmate when in Correctional Service Canada's custody. That is a big number, especially when compared to the $40 000 it costs to service a person out on parole. In addition, estimates provided by the correctional services commissioner indicated that the cost of building a new cell varied from $260 000 for a low-security unit to approximately $600 000 for a high-security cell. Had the Truth in Sentencing Act been in effect in 2007–08, it would have meant large expenditures. Federally, with stays of about 160 days longer on average than in provincial jails, an extra 3700 people would have been in the system, resulting in more than $600 million in additional funds spent annually on operations and capital expenditures (excluding new construction costs). New construction costs were estimated in the $350 million range per year over the next five years to build the cells necessary to accommodate growth in the number of inmates.

The second model picked up in greater detail the cost of building more facilities (with low, medium, high, and multi-level security) to accommodate more inmates. Since the lessening of the remand credit for time served meant that prisoners would have to serve longer sentences, it followed that more prisons would have to be built to accommodate them, since federal and provincial jails were already very crowded.

In addition, the provinces and territories would have to shoulder the costs of building more cells because the federal government had silently changed the Criminal Code, knowing that this outcome for provinces was inevitable. A tremendous amount of taxpayer money was at stake with this policy change. There was little or no debate on alternative policy strategies. No costings were provided to Parliament from the federal government until after we issued our report. Nothing showed up in adjustments to federal planned expenditures in the budget. These additional increases were notionally absorbed into the federal overall bottom line, which is no way to run a quarter-trillion-dollar annual enterprise. The Truth in Sentencing Act went into effect in February 2010.

Looking back, the entire episode illustrated perfectly how the Conservative government disregarded the principle of any meaningful fiscal accountability. Our elected representatives were expected to just buy into the government's rhetoric. Of course, the government added the political spin as well. When people questioned the agenda, they would be looked at as if they had two heads while being asked, "Are you not willing to be tough on crime?" Obviously, the optics could be tricky in such circumstances, so a lot of MPs kept their heads down. It was yet another example of the need for an independent PBO.

Another report that caused a stir concerned the Employment Insurance program. It raised many questions about the changing Canadian economy and the government's stimulus program to improve it. It also raised serious questions about how the new oversight board would impact the finances of the statutory program. In 2008, the federal government had changed the Financial Administration Act of Canada to create a new Crown corporation called the Canada Employment Insurance Financing Board (CEIFB). It was a good idea on paper; it would have been a good idea in normal times; but again, there are often troubles associated with that idea of normal. In this instance, the trouble was that the CEIFB would not last. Its principal task was to set premium rates for the Employment Insurance program and to manage fund balances in a responsible manner. It was set up with a $2 billion reserve in 2010, but was eventually dissolved in 2013 as the economic recession effectively pulled the rug out from under it. In periods of significant downturn, benefit payments to the unemployed rise and revenues slip. Deficits show up quickly in the account. The normal rules to adjust premium rates do not make sense. Finance ministers do not want taxes to rise when the economy is faltering because it will take purchasing power away from the marketplace when it is badly needed.

Jeff Danforth of the PBO told Parliament and Canadians in 2010 that the rug had been pulled out from under the newly minted CEIFB; he did not have to wait until 2013 to call its demise. The government had tied itself in knots with many unanswered questions about how the CEIFB would operate and survive. For instance, the government left Parliament and Canadians in the dark on how policy actions taken by the government in the 2009 Stimulus Budget would impact the finances of the CEIFB. What was going to happen to the $2 billion reserve? For example, the CEIFB would be explicitly compensated for the cost of the benefit enhancements announced in Budget 2009, but not for the cost of the premium rate freeze or the extension of benefits for long-tenured workers announced in Budget 2010.

Jeff maintained that the legislation governing the rate-setting mechanism had to be reconsidered to facilitate the implementation of the government's stimulus program. And, he made it clear in the analysis that the initial $2 billion reserve established with the newly minted Crown corporation was not enough. Within months of its creation, Jeff predicted that the CEIFB was basically dead in the water. History would prove him right, although it took another three years for the government to actually dissolve the board. While staffed with competent public servants and after spending some $5 million on operations, it could not make any claim to have had an impact on policy.

Jeff was a terrific PBO senior analyst. He ran PBO fiscal forecasts for a number of years and delivered work that may have embarrassed many of the fiscal analysts at the finance department. He was cool under pressure both inside and outside the office. The PBO report was transparent and analytical, far more so than the information produced by the government and new CEIFB. But in fairness to members of that board, they had their hands tied by the government right off the bat.

We released several more reports during our third year in quick order. One report examined differing estimates of economic potential output (Bank of Canada, IMF), which highlighted shortcomings, both in analysis and in transparency, of the documents prepared by Finance Canada. We made specific recommendations to improve and strengthen the finance documents so that members of Parliament could engage more effectively in the debate and scrutiny of fiscal policy at a historic time of global uncertainty. Rahm Emanuel, President Barack Obama's chief of staff during the president's first mandate, was famously quoted as saying, "You do not want to waste a good crisis." Our mission at the PBO was to promote fiscal transparency and fiscal analysis simultaneously. We had an important opportunity to expand the tool box for parliamentarians during the 2008–09 economic recession on both counts.

The challenge was, in a short period of time and with limited resources, to develop analytical tools that would stand the test of scrutiny by peers. We wanted these types of tools to be available for parliamentarians for use during their discussions with the minister of finance. We wanted parliamentarians to understand more than just what was happening to Canada's GDP as presented by Statistics Canada. Much more importantly, we wanted them to understand how the economy was performing relative to its potential—the so-called output gap. The latter was estimated assuming the economy was operating with labour and capital fully employed. When an economy is operating at full employment, it is like a car running smoothly on all its cylinders. When unemployment rates rise or capacity utilization rates fall, it is like a car whose cylinders are not functioning—performance and gas mileage are down. Like all estimates, they are subject to error and debate. Even the best mechanics sometimes struggle to figure out why a car isn't running as well as it should.

Mostafa Askari oversaw papers prepared by Chris Matier and Russ Barnett, two economists formerly from the Department of Finance. The PBO was able to tell parliamentarians and Canadians just how deep the recession was in 2009 as a result of their efforts. We made comparisons with previous recessions in Canada that had occurred during the 1980s and 1990s, and we encouraged finance minister Flaherty and others at finance to do the same kind of analysis of output gaps so we could compare estimates. The analysis showed that the depth of the recession was more akin to the recession we experienced in the early 1990s but not as deep as the steep recession in the early 1980s.

In Budget 2010, the finance department provided some estimates of potential output in a budget annex following up on a G20 commitment. Finance would provide this information to satisfy that commitment, but I've no doubt they felt little compulsion to provide it to Parliament otherwise. The comparative numbers showed that PBO and finance estimates moved in the same direction. Both estimates showed that this was a moderate and relatively U-shaped recession with the output gap remaining open until well into the medium term. (A word of explanation is in order here. Economists often talk about the shape of recessions. They are referring to the profile of output losses. V-shaped recessions have steep declines and quick recoveries. U-shaped recessions are highlighted by extended periods of relative weakness.

U-shaped recessions create special policy problems for our political leaders. For instance, durations of unemployment get longer. One outcome of this is that it becomes more difficult to get a job when someone is out of work for prolonged periods of time. Similarly, uncertainty about growth can impede investment decisions, which can weaken future growth.)

Chris, Jeff, and Russ were excellent economists and also a treat to watch as they interacted. There was constant trash-talking. They attacked each other on all fronts—from their skills to their wardrobes. Pat Brown had an office across the hallway and could often be heard laughing behind her computer as she listened to their goings on. Those three men provided tools for MPs and Canadians that the government and public service simply refused to provide. One such tool, the estimate of the output gap, was used in a debate to support the need for substantive stimulus—money that would fund infrastructure jobs and other initiatives across the country. That tool also helped deconstruct the nature of the ballooning federal deficit. It assisted in determining how much of this deficit was cyclical (and would be reduced when the economy returned to its potential) and how much of this deficit was structural (and would remain even when the economy got stronger).

Next came a report on the new Infrastructure Stimulus Fund suggesting that a significant number of projects were behind and had the potential to lose funding given the federal cost sharing rules and timelines. In response, the government suggested that we were off base and that everything was on track, yet they provided absolutely no supporting analysis for that position. It wouldn't be the last time we would get the brush-off on a recommendation while receiving no substantial analysis to support a position before Parliament. A lot of it looked like voodoo communications to me.

Finally, in the fall of 2010, we updated our economic outlook to incorporate what we referred to as the analysis of uncertainty. This important tool was developed by Chris Matier—the same person who had been informed earlier by a colleague that the PBO was a fledgling entity that had been set up to fail. In this instance, Chris incorporated the track record of average private sector outlooks in trying to determine a measure of uncertainty as it related to the economy. This tool had never been used in government finance documents and serves to provide a realistic perception of ability to project economic and fiscal outcomes. We expanded the PBO tool box so as to assist MPs to better understand the depth of a recession that was ongoing in an international context amid all of the fiscal challenges. Our medium-term outlook for the federal deficit was more pessimistic than that of the government's, which was not happy with our characterization of the aforementioned structural deficit problem. Oddly, they poured fuel on the fire themselves in part by reducing the GST rate.

We put out a series of reports with titles such as *Tough on Crime, Employment Insurance, Summit Security Costing,* and *Infrastructure Program.* These were all significant reports that the people in our office were proud to put their names to. At the same time, the rumour mill and gossipmongers were working at top speed. On any given day, we would hear that the PBO was about to be modified or mothballed or somehow vaporized. I'm sure that as time wore on some of our staff people must have become concerned about their jobs and future employability given that they were now going to be associated with a perceived government antagonist—yours truly! But if they were scared, I never knew it. On many occasions, I would sneak a peek into the open doors of the various offices and see analysts glued to screens full of numbers and lines. I would often witness an analyst drawing equations on a whiteboard, all the while being challenged and pushed by the commentary of a colleague who would be testing his or her work. Or I would hear Pat and Jocelyne Scrim (an administrative assistant with the PBO since 2010) conversing in an office, strategizing about how they were going to get the next project out the door. I would walk past the little kitchen around noon hour and often see six or more analysts huddled around a table, debating an issue or report with great enthusiasm. And then there was the laughter—always the laughter. They enjoyed each other's company and they enjoyed the stimulation that came out of those informal debates. I often referred to that group as my "kitchen cabinet," a title made famous by some of our former political leaders who worked to bring our Constitution home in 1982. There was energy everywhere. There was laughter and ease in the face of complexity and change. We had created an environment that was badly needed for the public service— open and transparent, lean and analytical.

As I reflect on those days at work, I remember something that happened during that trip we made to visit the Congressional Budget Office back in 2008. It was before we had released any reports or caused any stir in Ottawa. It was during the set-up period for our newly created office. I was in the office of economist Robert Reischauer who at the time was running the Urban Institute. Reischauer was a former director of the CBO and he regaled us with stories of the building of that office. He talked about the files they had completed and the legendary people he had worked with on some of those reports, including the likes of Alice Rivlin and Bob Sunshine. His words on that occasion were inspiring for me—his were the anecdotes of an energized public servant who had risen to serve that higher purpose. I promised myself at that moment that it would be those kinds of feelings—of energy, of inspiration—that I would attempt to inspire in leading the PBO. And it was happening.

We were now in our third year, mid-term in this experiment called the Parliamentary Budget Office with production ramped up and rolling. The product pipeline that we had envisioned back in year one was serving Canadians well.

But if I told you that I was prepared for what came next, I'd be a liar.

NINE

THE F-35 FIGHTER JET

More than any other issue, the controversy over a unique piece of military equipment—the F-35 fighter jet—would define my time as head of the PBO.

Most Canadians know that fighter aircraft have always been a big part of our military strategy and defence system, and successive governments in Ottawa had been studying the pros and cons of purchasing new fighter jets since the 1990s. Our aging F-18s had been in operation since the early 1980s, being deployed to assist NATO efforts in Bosnia, Libya, and elsewhere. What Canadians might not know is that the cost to replace a fleet of fighter planes, even for a relatively small military power such as Canada, costs tens of billions of dollars. And that kind of acquisition cannot happen overnight; replacing such a fleet is a slow process that takes many years. Prime Minister Harper's government decided to take action.

Defence Minister Peter MacKay, along with other senior government officials, settled on the new American-made F-35. On July 16, 2010, the government announced its intention to purchase sixty-five Lockheed Martin F-35 Lightning 11 aircraft, which it claimed was the only aircraft that could meet all of our national needs. Buying into the F-35 program would mean that

Canada would be in step with its American allies with a state-of-the-art piece of military hardware. Being able to coordinate with the Americans, the government argued, meant that any upgrades to the aircraft would be readily available to our air force pilots. It looked like a perfect fit and fix for our aging fleet of F-18s.

I cannot tell you how the government effectively costed out the entire program because we were never privy to such information. But what I can tell you is that once the decision was made to purchase the F-35s, the government produced and distributed a one-page document in the fall of 2010—yes, a *one-page* document that was supposed to provide costing estimates for the jets. Think about that in the context of our previously noted car example. Purchasing one car is a relatively minor undertaking when compared to buying sixty-five F-35s. Yet even when purchasing an auto, at the very least, most buyers would want a report detailing any potential problems before paying for that car. The federal government wasn't proposing to put out a few thousand dollars for a car; it was prepared to spend billions of taxpayer dollars on a fleet of fighter planes, but all it could muster was a one-page summary for members of Parliament with literally no supporting documentation. Governments throughout the ages have practised the art of manipulation to maintain power and get what they want, but in the case of the Conservative government's proposed purchase of the F-35s, the prime minister and his defence minister attempted to take manipulation to a whole new level.

The opposition parties were having none of it. Liberal MPs Ujjal Dosanjh from Vancouver and Dominic LeBlanc from Beauséjour requested that our office examine the proposed purchase once the government's lack of due diligence on the F-35 file became apparent. This was another project that we initially scrutinized with great care before accepting. Our report on the costs of the Afghanistan war had been difficult to produce given the lack of cooperation from the government, and we had no reason to believe that another military costing would be any easier. At one point during our F-35 deliberations, Ash Rajekar, my trusted colleague and a former defence service person in India himself, came into my office. He said, "Kevin, maybe we don't want to do this job. You have to be careful on this one. It could get really sticky. We won't be costing a social program here. This is the military. There are jobs and big money on the line. Some major companies have a huge stake in all of this." He was right there was a lot to gain or lose for many stakeholders. But my feeling was that this was the kind of project that our PBO was designed to undertake. It was an important decision with enormous economic and military repercussions. We felt compelled to tackle the job.

As head of the project, Tolga Yalkin's first task was to extract as much meaningful information from the Department of National Defence as possible. They were the people responsible for supplying the numbers on acquisition costs for the F-35 program to the government, and we wanted Parliament to have the benefit of the government's own detailed costing in whatever form that might take. Additionally, we requested that they release their data to us so we could reconcile it with our own PBO numbers. Only then would we be able to explain any potential differences between our numbers and the government's. But that wasn't going to happen—the DND wanted no part of our inquiries, and Tolga's requests fell on deaf ears. The only government data made available to us was the aforementioned one-page executive summary. We would have to go it alone.

It was a grind producing our report—as difficult as our costing of Canadian involvement in Afghanistan had been. Costing that war may have involved more moving parts, but in the case of the F-35 we were trying to cost a *moving target* in that the technology was continuing to change, making it extremely diffi-cult to arrive at a fixed cost. There was another big difference between Afghanistan and the F-35s. Remember, we had already been on the ground in Afghanistan for a number of years, so money had been spent already and there was at least a shadow of a paper trail for our analysts to use. Based on those numbers, we could make a reasonable forecast of future costs of our engage-ment there. But the still evolving F-35 was a different proposi-tion altogether: the government had already announced that it wanted this plane and our military was in agreement, but there was a dearth of information to support the purchase decision.

When we released our report on March 10, 2011, our forecast looked significantly different from the government's. We estimated that the F-35s would cost billions of dollars more than the government had projected in its one-page document—no small thing. The DND had pegged the number at $16 billion over a life-cycle of twenty years, with an acquisition cost of approxi-mately $75 million per plane, and a total of sixty-two planes to be purchased. We argued that the costing should have been done over a thirty-year timeline because, realistically, no one gets rid of planes after twenty years. Just look at how long our own F-18 fleet had remained in the air. Therefore, we estimated that a more realistic cost would be $30 billion over thirty years. Obviously, one of us was off base in our projections. We believed that our estimates were realistic because we were factoring in costs such as equipment upgrades over an extended period of time, which translates into big money. There might be two upgrades over the course of that additional ten-year time span in the thirty-year cycle. Those aspects of this acquisition had to be factored into the equation because that cost alone would translate into billions of dollars for taxpayers. We weren't the only people delivering that judgment. The accounting firm KPMG would eventually provide a forecast in line with what we were predicting.

What was the Harper government's response to these discrepancies? Their howls of protest centred around the fact that they had never done things that way in government before. That's quite an argument! The notion that forecasts should include not only the cost of acquisition but also maintenance costs over the life cycle of the planes had apparently never crossed their minds. That's not meant as sarcasm—it seems to accurately reflect their reality.

When we released our projected costs for the F-35s, all hell broke loose. The media figured out quickly that the emperor had no clothes when it came to purchasing fighter jets, and the F-35 procurement quickly became nightly news. "Budget officer, military trade shots over fighter jet costs" was one headline in *The Globe and Mail*.[1] "Jet lag: Some hard questions about the F-35 purchase," said the CBC.[2] At one point, the government and public service attacked the math that I had used in developing our estimates. Looking back, it still dumbfounds me that some of our politicians and public servants attempted to defend that which was not defensible in order to buy those jets. They wanted that plane at any cost, regardless of the impact on the public purse or the perception of good governance. But then, confidence and trust in government never seemed to be very high on their list of priorities.

---

[1] Murray Brewster, "Budget officer, military trade shots over fighter jet costs," *The Globe and Mail*, March 23, 2011, accessed May 10, 2015, at http://www.theglobeandmail.com/news/politics/budget-officer-military-trade-shots-over-fighter-jet-costs/article4266664.

[2] Brian Stewart, "Jet lag: Some hard questions about the F-35 purchase," CBC News, March 23, 2011, accessed May 10, 2015, at http://www.cbc.ca/news/world/jet-lag-some-hard-questions-about-the-f-35-purchase-1.1089891.

Over time it had become painfully obvious that more discussion and examination of the entire F-35 purchase was required. The media would not let the issue die easily. The fighter jet procurement had become a critical project on multiple levels involving multiple groups and organizations.

While the F-35 was attracting most of the headlines during the ensuing months, which led to the ongoing delay in the government's procurement decision, other government business still had to be addressed. I attended many committee meetings during this time in an attempt to explain some of our PBO reports. At one of them in late April 2012, I spoke about our projections on the economic outlook to the finance committee. Frankly, on that occasion I stunk the joint out. It had not been my best effort. I had allowed several Conservative backbenchers to do a thorough job of obscuring the issues as well as our analysis at that meeting. They would use most of their allotted time setting up the question, which meant that there was little time left for me to answer. I felt that I had let the team down. Confidence in our methodologies was on the line. That kind of performance couldn't happen again, especially when I knew that sooner or later I would be talking about the F-35. And it would be sooner rather than later.

At the same time, the government and DND were also walking a tightrope on the F-35 procurement. Both needed to demonstrate their competence as fiscal managers, and there was a long list of potential military procurements waiting to be addressed. If the government couldn't successfully navigate the F-35 purchase, there would be more doubt when it came to future purchases of ships, military vehicles, and other materials. The opposition parties had a stake in all of this, too, as they had fought and lost a general election on the theme of the government's lack of transparency and trust.

The government's credibility on the F-35 then took another big hit. Auditor General Michael Ferguson, the man who had replaced Sheila Fraser as AG, released a scathing report on the F-35 procurement on April 3, 2012. In it he indicated that the Harper government had in its possession numbers for the F-35 life cycle costs that were even larger than those we had predicted at the PBO. In spite of that information, the government and key members of the public service had continued to attack and attempt to discredit PBO numbers and analysis. It was a stunning revelation. Suddenly, the opposition parties had the scent of a smoking gun.

Shortly after my poor performance at the finance committee, I was summoned to attend a public accounts committee meeting on May 3, 2012. This was a gathering designed to assess the potential F-35 purchase in light of the auditor general's recent findings. I could ill afford to stumble again. Our strategy was to focus on our own PBO report, not the report that the AG had tendered. That might seem counterintuitive given that the AG had basically endorsed our numbers, but we wanted to focus on our own projections because ours had the added benefit of having been peer-reviewed by experts. That counts for something. At the meeting, everyone was seated at the huge rectangular table with the media and staffers packed into the back rows. There was one moment when MP Chris Alexander said something to the effect that this was the way the DND normally presented numbers—on a twenty-year life cycle. I responded—and it is on the record—that just because it was normal does not mean it is right or correct. Certain realities came to light very quickly. The operational costs for the F-35 were expected to be higher than those of the F-18 for good reason, and this was accepted and estimated by colleagues in the United States. Still, the government kept doggedly repeating its story for all to hear. I've often wondered how men and women could sit through those types of briefings, *knowing* that their government is dead wrong, and yet still remain silent. And that's the problem with Ottawa. MPs knew that they didn't have nearly enough detail to make a decision on such a huge purchase. Still, many sat mute, not prepared to voice any such concerns. It isn't exactly a shining example of how democratically elected officials should act. As our PBO contingent left the committee room, there were some delicate moments, glances, and exchanges with both members of Parliament and the public service. I remember specifically looking at Tom Ring, an assistant deputy minister of public procurement, who seemed as if he were walking into a lion's den. After all, at many of these kinds of meetings, very few people showed up. But here he was entering the equivalent of the Roman Colosseum—and it was standing room only. Many of these men and women were old colleagues. Some were now coming into the room in an attempt to defend the public service position, but the position was untenable. Seeing some of their faces, I felt at once angry and somewhat empathetic as well—they were expected to be good foot soldiers. The man I had replaced at finance all those years ago, Robert Fonberg, entered the room at the same time that I was leaving. He never came near me and seemed almost to go out of his way to avoid me. "Status quo," I thought—this was all business. I knew what his take on the F-35 purchase was going to be: he would back the government position, so there was no need to stay and hear his response. It was then that I stepped out into the hallway right into the media scrum and the glare of television cameras—a different kind of lion's den. And that is when my exchange occurred with Julie Van Dusen about the F-35 boondoggle and the government's credibility: "Are you suggesting that the government wanted Canadians to think that these planes would cost a lot less money?" "Yes."

Here, I need to make a brief confession. Global TV anchor Kevin Newman told me afterward that my slight hesitation before answering Van Dusen's question—that pregnant pause where I looked over my shoulder for a brief moment—had been a real stroke of genius. He thought it had been scripted on my part. Some perceived that I was attempting to show up the prime minister, pretending to see if he could hear what I was about to say. Of course, this was on national television and not behind closed doors. Others thought that I was looking for some kind of legal counsel before answering the question. Actually, I don't even remember making that gesture. What really happened was that my colleague, Mostafa Askari, tugged at my jacket sleeve just as Van Dusen asked her question. I don't believe that Mostafa had heard the question; he was simply trying to get my attention so we could wrap things up. I turned in his direction for a split second, and when I turned back toward the camera, I answered the question. So there was no grand plan in that scrum, no attempt to imply anything more, or insult anyone, or try to add a moment of drama. Of course, in such an atmosphere, rife with political grandstanding I suppose it's not surprising that some would choose to believe that it was intentional.

When I returned to the office after that televised scrum, I immediately ran into Chris Matier, who looked as if he had just seen a ghost. He feared that I'd just loaded a gun for the government to kill us with, and said, "Kev, they are going to fire you. You can't accuse the government of misleading." When I said I was just telling the truth, he responded, "Yeah, you're right. But you're still going to get fired." When I got home that night, my wife Julie said, "Wow, you had quite the day. You're all over the news." She told me that she had been watching *Power and Politics* and that the CBC's political panel of journalists had replayed my little hesitation move a couple of times while having a good chuckle. Later that evening I received an email in very legalistic language from the parliamentary librarian informing me that my use of the word *mislead* was not appropriate. I also received numerous congratulatory emails and letters from many Canadian citizens over the next several days. One letter came from an old colleague, Harvey Sims, a retired civil servant who told me how proud he was of me for telling the truth. That letter meant an awful lot to me. In the end, although my wrists got slapped, I didn't really believe that my actions could justify the government taking away my job. At least, I didn't think it would happen that day.

There is another important aspect to the F-35 affair that needs mentioning as well. The controversy over the fighter plane occurred during our fourth year of operation. By then, the PBO had become entrenched and accepted in Ottawa in most quarters. But in spite of what some government officials might have tried to spin, we never envisioned ourselves as policy makers. That was the jurisdiction of elected officials. If the government of the day decided to buy fighter jets, so be it. If they decided that war was in the best interest of our country and those jets would be a major part of that decision, so be it. If they could convince enough people that we needed to include mud wrestling as a national sport, and everyone bought in, then let the games begin. No one at the PBO *ever* attempted to pre-empt or tamper with the elected government's agenda. My job as the parliamentary budget officer was simply to ensure that all Canadians were receiving the best numbers behind the various policies and programs. I didn't say the *correct* numbers; I said the *best* numbers. Many senior members of the media remarked to me in private that our F-35 data made for a very strong and clear report. They knew it, so I can only assume that many MPs must have known that as well. Yet, at that public accounts committee meeting, most sat stone faced and said nothing. That meeting could have been a historic moment for the government, a moment in which they collectively could have said, "Hold it, we got this wrong. We need to make this right." Instead, some civil servants and politicians chose to hide, confuse, obfuscate, and try to deceive the entire country. The people in that room should have acknowledged that the information from the AG report was damning. Instead, it took Julie Van Dusen to ask, outside in the hallway, the question that should have been asked within that meeting room. But no one had the guts to do that. The mistrust was underscored by the hypocrisy. It was a scene I will never forget, a low point in the recent history of our democracy.

At the time of this writing, the F-35 procurement remains a mess. There has been no purchase, yet many rumours persist. One story being circulated has the Conservative government committed to an initial purchase of three of the jets. There's a murkiness about the entire process, with government representatives muddying the waters even further and more than a few bodies having been thrown overboard. The F-35 remains a topic that is unresolved, though the headlines have subsided. How will it all eventually turn out? Your guess is as good as mine, though my gut tells me that the federal government is unlikely to broach the topic of F-35 procurement in advance of the 2015 federal election. I doubt they'll kick that hornet's nest.

TEN

PBO AND POLITICS COLLIDE—
THE ELECTION OF 2011

The F-35 episode led to some dramatic procedural and political outcomes early in 2011 that no one could have envisioned. And in the process, Prime Minister Harper and his government would be taken to task.

The government continued to dodge our requests for information on a wide range of subjects. In the case of the F-35, we hadn't been able to pry anything from the DND specifically. But it went beyond just one issue. During 2010–11, suddenly the federal government was running a big deficit, as opposed to the long run of surplus budgets that had been the norm. The economy had been greatly weakened, yet the government still wanted to slash corporate income tax rates, to move forward on expensive military purchases, and to expand the prison system, although no one in government would go public with any financial analysis on those major issues. Instead, MPs were asking us to do costings. After all, I was their budget officer. I had been told by the speakers of both Houses that my office shouldn't find itself in the middle of major issues and debates, but the reality was that we were in up to our necks whether we wanted it or not. MPs were demanding help, and we knew that to become involved was the right thing to do. And members of

Parliament had finally arrived at the point where they had had enough. After all, the duty of any MP who is not part of the prime minister's cabinet in our parliamentary system is to hold the government to account, and our duty at the PBO was to provide MPs with the data necessary to perform theirs.

It was time for some drastic action. I requested Tolga's legal advice about options we might have to assist MPs, and he and Sahir developed a plan in which we would invoke the authority of the House of Commons Standing Committee on Finance to request the needed information on behalf of the PBO. The strategy is a testament to Tolga's legal expertise, his knowledge of how government works in our country, and his intestinal fortitude. That type of request would engage parliamentary privilege and it would include a provision to send for persons, papers, and records. It would be much tougher for the government to duck the finance committee than to skirt the PBO. Tolga drafted a request and some members of the finance committee worked with our staff to refine the wording. PBO staff knew how to frame an information request. After all, we were all former public servants from central agencies responsible for budgeting, and this was our business. The final version was handed over to the finance committee, where it was voted on and formally adopted. The request was then forwarded to the various responsible ministers and departments within the government—Minister Flaherty for finance requests, Minister Toews for crime legislation data, etc.

The request went out in December 2010, but again, the government responded with only limited information. And in the case of requests for F-35 data, this time the DND dredged up "national security" as the rationale for their lack of full disclosure. Their response fell short in the eyes of some members of the finance committee, who asked the PBO to look at the government responses and comment on the level of compliance. We were given three weeks to complete that task.

On information related to corporate profits and income taxes, we noted that the government had complied. We were now in a position to provide Parliament with analysis on the government's fiscal forecast, including projections on the tax base, effective tax rates and revenues, and reconciliations with the PBO numbers. This was good, but it was no victory for Parliament. It turned out that much of this information had already been shared with private sector forecasters in past years to assist them with their own forecasts. How ironic—the private sector was receiving more detailed information than elected representatives were.

On the issue of crime bills and the F-35, the government's responses were inadequate. They provided very few metrics; it was next to impossible to understand incremental costs and fiscal impact; and there was little to no cost analysis. The government and the public service were effectively thumbing their respective noses at Parliament, as if such numbers somehow really did not matter. Or perhaps their view was that somehow the figures weren't required by members of Parliament. In this, there is yet another piece of irony, since within our system of governance, it is the House of Commons that provides the authority for the government to spend. Our assessment was unequivocal: the government and public service had fallen short on their responses. We sent our report to the finance committee and also posted the findings on our website, as was our policy.

The government's refusal to comply with full disclosure was reviewed by the Standing Committee on Procedure and House Affairs—a serious development. I was called to appear before that committee on March 16, 2011; Mostafa and Sahir were at my side during that meeting. This was battle's front line, and we were right in the line of fire. Sahir would sometimes quote from the movie *Apocalypse Now*, the scene where a macho military commando stands on the beach in a theatre of war and says, "I love the smell of napalm in the morning." He'd say it because we always knew we would be heading into crossfire between opposition members and government backbenchers—and Sahir loved all of it. He used that line a lot in the fall of 2010 and in the early months of 2011. He used it again on March 16 as well.

As we sat there in the committee meeting, I knew that we had earned some credibility with many of the people in the room. We weren't hiding from anyone. Our numbers were there for everyone to see. Here are my verbatim comments from that meeting as recorded in *Hansard*.[3]

> I have a few brief opening remarks based on the Parliamentary Budget Officer report dated February 25, 2011, entitled *Analysis of Government Responses to a Motion of the House of Commons Standing Committee on Finance*.
>
> My views on the provision of financial information and analysis to Parliament are shaped by three points. First, the Parliament of Canada owes a fiduciary duty to the Canadian people to control public monies on their behalf. Canada's Constitution established and affirms this duty. Second, to assist in the fulfillment of this duty, the Parliament of Canada, through the Accountability Act in December 2006, created the position of the Parliamentary Budget Officer and tasked him or her with providing independent and transparent analysis on

[3] Parliament of Canada, Standing Committee on Procedure and House Affairs, minutes of meeting held March 16, 2011, accessed May 10, 2015, at http://www.parl.gc.ca/HousePublications/Publication.aspx?DocId=5045004.

economic trends, the nation's finances, the estimates, and costing. In order to provide such analysis to Parliament, the Parliamentary Budget Officer needs access to financial and related information and analysis contained within the government's Expenditure Management System. This information and analysis is routinely collected, generated, and presented by government departments and central agencies.

PBO analysis of documents provided by the government to the House of Commons Standing Committee on Finance, and tabled on February 17, 2011, in the House of Commons, addressed three issues: first, the estimated costs of the planned reduction of corporate income tax rates; second, the incremental costs to the fiscal framework of the government's justice legislation; and, third, the estimated cost of the F-35 aircraft.

From a PBO perspective, with respect to corporate profits and tax revenues, the government has provided an adequate response to the finance committee request. In addition to projected income components such as corporate profits, personal income, etc., parliamentarians are advised to ask the government to provide underlying assumptions in all future annual budgets and updates.

Second, with respect to justice legislation, the government has not provided an adequate response to the finance committee request. Again, Chair, we have not seen the information tabled today, but the government has not provided an adequate response to the finance committee request.

Full compliance with the request requires clarity around the projected cost estimates, such as whether they are incremental or presented on a cash or accrual basis; a breakdown of costs between operating and capital for all information provided; details of the government's underlying methodologies, assumptions, cost drivers, and risk; and basic statistics, such as head counts, annual flows, and unit costs per inmate, per employee, and per new cell construction.

A modest example of the nature and extent of such compliance might be found in the PBO report entitled "The Funding Requirement and Impact of the 'Truth in Sentencing Act' on the Correctional System in Canada."

Third, with respect to the proposed acquisition of the F–35 joint strategic fighter, which was included in the original FINA [Standing Committee on Finance] motion, the government has not provided an adequate response to the finance committee request. Full compliance with the request requires details of the government's underlying methodologies, assumptions, cost drivers, and risks; documents related to acquisition and life cycle costs; and an explanation as to why new or unplanned sources of funds from the fiscal framework will not be needed to fund the new purchase.

A modest example of the nature and extent of such compliance might be found in the PBO's report entitled "An Estimate of the Fiscal Impact of Canada's Proposed Acquisition of the F–35 Lightning II Joint Strike Fighter."

That reference in the last paragraph was my own little dig at the government. The PBO had already prepared data on the F–35 for publication. Where was their data?

I told committee members—including the chair, Joe Preston, and vice chairs Claude DeBellefeuille and Yasmin Ratansi—that everything requested by the finance committee was absolutely essential for MPs to do their jobs. I also noted that this information, according to the government's own treasury board policy, MUST exist. The next day, March 17, we tabled a report to show that the government's additional information from the previous day was still insufficient to provide parliamentarians with enough data to make the best possible choices. The Standing Committee on Procedure and House Affairs agreed with our assertions—and it would make that known in a dramatic fashion.

On March 21, 2011, the committee tabled its report in the House of Commons, declaring that the government was in contempt of Parliament. This was unprecedented, as no previous federal government in this country had ever been found in contempt of Parliament. The government had attempted to ignore the law, and the opposition parties had seen enough. Four days later, the House passed a motion of "no confidence" and within days the minority Harper government fell.

Our intention hadn't been to play a role in bringing down the government. Rather, we had just wanted their numbers, but they consistently refused all requests. Based upon his legal expertise and understanding of how Parliament functions, Tolga had done the only thing he felt was open to our office. That strategy triggered other events that led to a federal election being called for May 2, 2011.

One has to wonder why the government would even risk contempt of Parliament charges, knowing that it could lead to an election. Conservatives were prepared to take a great gamble without having any guarantee of a positive outcome. And there were some amazing results from the election of 2011. Harper emerged unscathed from the contempt of Parliament actions.

But more than that, and to the surprise of many analysts and political pundits, his Conservative Party won a majority government. The Liberals would win the fewest seats in their history, ushering in the speedy demise of their leader, Michael Ignatieff. And Elizabeth May, the leader of the Green Party, would make history by becoming the first member of that party to win a seat in the House of Commons.

There have been many theories as to how Harper managed to win the 2011 election in such a sweeping manner. I believe the majority win for Prime Minister Harper was the result of a couple of factors. The stimulus package, which had been implemented at the behest of Parliament in 2009–10, bought a lot of goodwill across the country during those turbulent and difficult economic times. In addition, the communications people for the Conservatives did a masterful job of portraying Canada as a country that had not been devastated by the recession of 2008. This feat implied strong fiscal leadership, and the government touted that line during the election. I also believe that the majority win after the contempt of Parliament charge unfortunately validated the government's own apparent belief that Parliament itself could be bypassed, and I've no doubt that the election outcome has helped perpetuate the unaccountability that had been and continues to be the hallmark of this government.

One of my favourite economists is the late Hyman Minsky, who wrote *Stabilizing an Unstable Economy*, a prescient book often cited after the 2008 financial crisis. Minsky theorized that if a crisis is successfully contained, then risky practices are "validated." He would argue that this would set the stage for subsequent crises that could be more severe. My fear was and still is that the 2011 election results validated the secretiveness of the federal government and public service. That may pave the way for more severe transparency problems in the future. In essence, the voters of Canada endorsed the government leaders' bad behaviour. And that behaviour has not changed. This is not a political comment solely about the Conservatives and the public service, but a comment on the condition of all governments in Canada, and it represents a dangerous precedent.

ELEVEN
A BATTLE FOR TRANSPARENCY

With a majority win in the 2011 election, Prime Minister Harper and colleagues released a new budget when Parliament reconvened. Budget 2012 was much anticipated for two important reasons. First, given the Conservative majority victory, there were some observers (including yours truly) who wondered if government officials might change their approach and become more open in the way their government conducted business. The hopeful argument was that now, with a majority, maybe they could relax a little—be more transparent, more willing to debate. Second, the government had made a strong commitment in the election campaign to achieve fiscal balance over the next five years. The question was, how fast and hard would the government put on the fiscal brakes? The economy was growing but it was hardly a stellar increase; restraint would only slow any economic recovery. On the other hand, there is an old political adage that if a government is going to have to dish out tough medicine during its mandate, it is best to front-end load the pain for the electorate. By the time the next election comes around, governments want all the tough stuff behind them.

What we learned in Budget 2012 was that the government reaffirmed its commitment to fiscal restraint in spite of a weak economy. Direct program spending, a little less than half of spending for all programs, would be frozen for five years. The government would indeed use old political tactics—the tough medicine would come early. In addition, it would create a budget day smokescreen. To move the debate away from the impact of austerity on food inspection services or the Coast Guard or seniors, the government announced that it was ready to get rid of the penny. The media focused on the penny issue and downplayed the austerity issue. It was a clever move by the Conservative government.

In the lead-up to the budget, the Conservative government made some critical decisions that would have an impact on Canada's long-term financial health. While officials argued other-wise, they behaved as if they had indeed created a structural deficit and needed to do something about it. The communica-tions team in the Prime Minister's Office, in conjunction with the minister of finance, went on the offensive. They wanted to highlight that Canada was economically outperforming other G8 countries. They saw an opportunity to collectively beat their chests while claiming that our recession was not as severe as other countries were experiencing. And this was in part true. Canada did not have as severe a financial crisis as the United States and many parts of Europe. We did not lose any banks. Our problems had been created from outside our own borders, but we were still hurting in a big way. Canadian unemployment rates were elevated. Many industries were operating well below capacity. At this time, Finance Minister Flaherty stated that the PBO's economic and fiscal forecasts were more pessimistic than those of the private sector and international organizations such as the IMF.

Those accusations prompted Chris Matier, Russ Barnett, and Jeff Danforth, under the leadership of Mostafa, to take a close look at the IMF and PBO forecasts. Over the next five years, the

IMF had projections for federal deficits very much in line with PBO projections (actually a little higher) and more notably higher than those emanating from the Department of Finance. Also, and very importantly, the IMF provided independent estimates of the output gap (where the economy was operating relative to its potential) and the structural budget balance (what the federal budget balance would be if the economy was operating at its potential). The minister of finance would not permit finance officials to publicly release their own estimates to Parliament and Canadians. I can only conclude that he would not do so because it would shed light on the reality that our economy was struggling, even though it was growing marginally. In addition, I've no doubt that neither the prime minister nor the finance minister wanted any light shone on the fact that the federal deficit had a structural component to it which had been created in large part by government policies. For instance, cuts to the GST, along with lowered personal and corporate income tax rates, left us with a revenue shortfall that would not balance the books even when the economy was operating at near to full capacity. Again, the IMF estimates reinforced the PBO message that the Canadian economy was slowly digging itself out of a large hole (an output gap of about four percentage points in 2009) and about half the federal deficit was structural in nature.

Finance Minister Flaherty had vehemently denied that there was any structural deficit. We maintained that there was indeed a systemic problem that created a relatively small but undeniably structural deficit. The IMF was confirming that as well. It was the same IMF that the minister of finance would quote in saying that we were doing better than other countries. But that was only half correct. While the finance minister would deny the presence of a structural deficit, he would commit to spending restraint in future budgets. That action suggested that the deficit required special measures so that his government could balance the federal books before the 2015 election. Our people exposed some of the "inconvenient truths" that our government seems to continually try to sidestep.

In addition, we released another major fiscal sustainability report in September 2011 that added the provincial government dimension. The analysis highlighted longer term fiscal gaps (such as the ability to stabilize debt to GDP) at both the federal and provincial levels. The provincial gap largely reflected rising health-care spending. The federal finance minister announced to the provinces at a meeting of federal–provincial finance ministers on December 19, 2011, that the escalator for the Canada Health Transfer was going to be cut in half, to the tune of $30 billion between 2017 and 2024. Instead of the Canada Health Transfer growing by six percent annually, it would now grow by an average of the growth rate in the economy. PBO analysis indicated that with this move, the longer term fiscal sustainability gap at the federal level would be eliminated, but the gap at the provincial level would grow. In essence, Ottawa was handing over the health care spending issue and the entire spectre of aging demographics to the provinces. It would seem that it will increasingly be the provinces' issue to solve.

In January 2012, Prime Minister Harper went to Davos, Switzerland, to attend the World Economic Forum, a prestigious gathering of leading economists, politicians, and business trend-setters on the world economic stage. Out of the blue at the conference, the PM announced in a speech that the age eligibility for the Old Age Security (OAS) program in Canada would have to rise from age sixty-five to age sixty-seven. This was a shocking revelation for many people back home, including everyone at the PBO. The announcement seemed to come out of left field. At the PBO we could find no hard analysis provided by the government to support their position that it was necessary to raise the age of eligibility. Yet, the PM declared that the program was not sustainable.

We decided to do our own analysis, supported by an additional analysis from the chief actuary. A month later, we indicated that, based on our methodology, the federal fiscal structure was sustainable. And that meant that the Old Age Security program was sustainable as well. That report was discussed and debated, both in Parliament and in the press. Seniors' groups from across the country started to demand information. I thought at the time that had my father still been alive, he would not have been happy with this situation. I doubt he would have taken kindly to the notion of shovelling potash for another two years after his sixty-fifth birthday. That hadn't been the deal he had worked and lived under all his life.

The government kept trying to avoid the real issues associated with its OAS pronouncement by calling my competence into question. They attempted to paint me as an attack dog that was opposed to the government's policy. In fact, we were attacking the *fiscal aspects of the policy*, the *economics behind their policy*. As had been the pattern, no one in the government produced any meaningful fiscal analysis to counter our findings. The auditor general released a report saying the federal government should do a sustainability analysis. Interestingly, once the AG issued his recommendation, finance officials released findings on the very same day to their website. They basically stated exactly what we at the PBO had already released. Suddenly, the government was proclaiming and validating our data, though not showing the likely impact on provincial budgets or on pensions that we had included. It all left me scratching my head.

It was early February in 2012. I was sitting at the food court at the World Exchange Plaza in Ottawa, having a bowl of soup from Claudio the Soup Guy. Suddenly, flashing across one of the television screens within viewing range, Finance Minister Flaherty's tense face appeared. Then an unflattering photo of yours truly showed up on the screen as well. Flaherty's demeanour began to make sense. "I wonder if it was something I said," I thought to myself. Then the finance minister shared with the general public his verdict on my abilities. Three words: "Unbelievable, unreliable, and incredible." It's hard to describe what it feels like to be singled out on national television as incompetent, but I had almost grown used to the personal attacks. It was yet another salvo that had nothing to do with the issues or actual economics of the matter at hand. It had all become so predictable, it was almost laughable. I learned to first endure and then eventually enjoy some of his more colourful commentary. He was a hell of a politician who knew how to play the game in Ottawa. Later, we had T-shirts made up for the office staff with those words stencilled across the front. Yes, there was some "unbelievable, unreliable, and incredible" information being provided to the Canadian people but it sure wasn't coming from my office.

When we showed up at our regular fall meeting with the House finance committee, many Conservative backbenchers thought we were committing a type of heresy for moving away from the typical private sector outlook for growth. In the spring, we had predicted sluggish growth due to a weak global economy and the government's policy of fiscal restraint. Now, those Conservative backbenchers were very quiet. I reminded them in my opening remarks that private sector Canadian forecasts were being revised down to PBO numbers just in case they were suffering from economic amnesia. Our office also estimated the drag on the economy that resulted from federal fiscal restraint. We were not against fiscal restraint: we just wanted MPs to realize that, in such situations, there are always policy trade-offs. We were cutting spending in a weak economy to get rid of a structural deficit created by the Conservative government. Finance Minister Flaherty would never acknowledge the negative impact of restraint on the economy, or the presence of the structural deficit. Yet PBO analysts were exposing those realities to members of Parliament.

Another reality we wanted to explore was the sustainability of the Canada and Quebec Pension Plans (CPP and QPP). The ensuing work meant that the PBO had the most complete picture of fiscal sustainability in the country. It was not provided by the minister of finance for parliamentarians, however. To do the job, the team worked with the very competent and professional office of the chief actuary. Canada is blessed with some extremely gifted global public servant leaders. Mark Carney is probably the best known, for his work on central banking in Canada and in the United Kingdom. Julie Dickson and her predecessor, Nick Le Pan, are also recognized worldwide for their superior work as superintendents of our financial institutions. Their leadership helped ensure we did not have a financial meltdown in 2008. In my view, Canada's chief actuary, Jean-Claude Ménard, is another global leader. He is the kind of person we want supervising our pensions.

We had looked at changes to funding health care, Old Age Security, and program spending restraint and concluded that our federal fiscal structure was sustainable, even with the challenge of an aging population. Now we affirmed the chief actuary's analysis that our pensions were currently sustainable, but we highlighted a fiscal gap that needed to be addressed at the provincial and territorial level of governments. This set up a debate at committee on the issue of fiscal sustainability for our country. As Canadians, we all need to keep in mind that without meaningful analysis from independent sources, there can be no meaningful debate. It is safe to suggest that the entire sustainability issue will heat up again during the 2015 election. Our health care and pension issues are far from being solved at this moment. Political leaders have kicked the can down the road. We do not have the policies and funding arrangements in place to control health care costs in the future. Most Canadians do not have access to private pension plans. We have not saved enough to support our retirements.

TWELVE
THESE NUMBERS DON'T ADD UP

If pensions were an important issue for Canadians, two other areas also affected the public purse: public sector compensation and ship procurement. Both received big play in the media across the country, and both are important for Canadians to consider. They amount to tens of billions of dollars.

Given their $43 billion price tag, public service wages and benefits need to be scrutinized for taxpayers. Citizens who are footing the bill should have an understanding of how and where their money is being spent. The genesis of this report was both personal and professional. It had been approximately ten years since the public service had prepared a major report on the state of the civil service in Canada. That report had been produced by an old colleague of mine, Jim Lahey, while we were both at the Treasury Board of Canada Secretariat. Jim prepared an excellent piece which was subsequently basically buried by the bureaucracy and lost in the shuffle of different political transitions between prime ministers from Chrétien to Martin to Harper. Jim did a solid job of running many red flags up the pole, which suggested at the time that the wage envelope was becoming significantly more expensive. He surmised that it could be better managed as well. Unfortunately, his observations fell largely on deaf ears.

I met with Jim for lunch about a year into my mandate as PBO, and shared with him my feeling that the time had come for the PBO to pick up where he had left off. As someone who had been on the inside, I understood as well as anyone on the Hill that past prime ministers and finance ministers were often not briefed properly on trends and issues about public service data. Collective bargaining was centrally managed out of the Treasury Board, yet deputy ministers ran the show with respect to hiring. Reporting to the prime minister was usually focused on wage settlements and largely missed developments to changes in employment levels and the rapid growth in benefits. Over three decades of work in Ottawa, I had witnessed the big swings firsthand; they seemed somewhat cyclical during my time as a civil servant—it was always either feast or famine. Whenever a deficit would rear its ugly head, the politicians in power would pound their desks and look to cut back on the public service. That kind of show always made for good headlines. But if a surplus suddenly saw the light of day, then look out—we could not hire new civil servants fast enough. There was no apparent vision as to what the public service should be in size and scope and no way to effectively manage such a large enterprise. There was no real paymaster watching the overall changes in the wage scales either. Overall, the compensation system for the public sector was, at best, inconsistent.

Sahir had recently hired a young analyst from Environment Canada, Jessica Strauss, who had a unique background, having been trained both as an architect at McGill and then as a financial analyst at Cornell University. I made the pitch to Sahir and Jessica that we needed a report on public sector compensation—admittedly not an easy undertaking. We initially struggled with the potential scope of the project: aside from the sheer size of the wage envelope, there were no annual reports on compensation to track. Over time, the public service had become very effective at not being particularly transparent, and the civil service had become coated in a kind of teflon—nothing ever seemed to stick. I could not think of another program that possessed less big-picture analysis than that of public service compensation. As the team worked on this file, I knew we would be putting the PBO right in the line of fire with the public service. I was the one asking for this data, not an MP. This one would hit close to home—right in the personal bank accounts of the public service.

It took almost a year to get the report finished and released, and during that time, Jessica Strauss taught all of us "old dogs" a lesson in perseverance. It was a struggle to collect the data. When we were ready to go public, the timing could not have been better. Budget 2012 indicated plans to eliminate approximately 19 000 jobs from a 350 000-strong civil service. In typical fashion, the government and public service had offered little to no analysis on the nature of the cutbacks and their potential impact. You didn't have to be a genius to know that if the government was planning to freeze spending, it was going to have to flatten the public sector compensation. The early communications emanating from the government about these cuts were that nobody had to worry; it could all be done through attrition. That meant that older civil servants (such as yours truly) would soon be retiring from the public service and the government would not rehire for those vacated positions. I'm sure the prime minister and finance minister would have enjoyed seeing me leave sooner rather than later, along with many other retirement-ready civil servants. But there was going to have to be a substantial exodus if they were intending to reduce the public sector so as to meet their stated fiscal objectives. Those numbers simply didn't add up.

The question that kept coming up in our office was, why did the government not lay out a human resources plan for its austerity objectives? I felt there were two possible reasons for this lack of clarity. One, they did not have a plan. It was possible they believed that it could all be managed by the deputy ministers with little risk to programs and services. Two, and more politically interesting, the Conservatives occupied a number of seats that belonged to ridings within the Ottawa Valley. Naturally, you are probably going to have more than a cursory number of public servants living in those ridings. Put it all together and it means that a lot of negative publicity about the cutbacks could not help their chances in the 2015 general election in those Ottawa Valley ridings. Conservative seats could be lost as a result, and the election outcome could hang in the balance. Looking back, I think it was probably a little of both. Professional politicians tend to act or react with specific outcomes always envisioned—political and otherwise.

By this time, there was a media thirst for information that needed to be quenched. Jessica's report highlighted the average compensation at about $114 000 per public servant. This struck many people as a big number, especially since it was well above average industrial wages. At first I was questioned and then criticized for appearing to have inflated the number by including those "all-in" public service benefits. I made it clear that we needed the total compensation number to properly assess all contributors to the monetary well-being that came with a public service job, which included health benefits such as drug and dental insurance. The number reflected this "all-in" comprehensive summary.

Jessica's analysis illuminated the large swings in public sector compensation over the past two decades. The graphs looked like a roller coaster ride, with major restraint in the 1990s followed by major expansion up to the 2012 budget. The PBO work suggested that the Conservative government's plan was to reverse the growth of recent years. This would be essential if the government was serious about its balanced budget fiscal target for 2015.

The Strauss report also showed that over the past two decades, federal public service compensation had outpaced the private sector and provincial levels of government as well. It was hard data and difficult for anyone to argue with. Nonetheless, the report received criticism from the office of the president of the Treasury Board. There were insinuations that the PBO had used incorrect figures, but the reality is that we used publicly available data from the receiver general of Canada. We had also had many discussions behind the scenes with Treasury Board analysts, many of whom were my old colleagues, as we wanted to be sure that we were making appropriate "apples to apples" comparisons with other sectors. As with most other major PBO reports, the government and public service did not respond with any type of analytical paper or commentary. They must have just hoped that eventually it would all go away. But the day after the report was released, Jessica's work appeared on the front pages of the *Ottawa Citizen* newspaper and other papers across the country.

One of the last major reports involved the costing of joint support ships (JSS). As a budget officer, whenever you hear the words "strategy," "procurement," and "$40 billion," your ears perk up. In June of 2010, the government had announced a very large procurement effort known as the National Shipbuilding Procurement Strategy. It included the construction of combat and noncombat ships and a number of small ships for our Department of National Defence and Coast Guard. The total acquisition value was estimated by the government to be close to $40 billion, and the work was expected to be undertaken by

Canadian shipyards over the next twenty to thirty years. There was a lot of excitement around this effort, given the need for new ships and the potential economic spinoffs for our coastal regions which had shipyards hungry for work. Also, there was a sense that the government and public service got off to a good start by running a fair process for shipyard selection.

Military procurement is a particularly expensive and risky venture. Inevitably, there are design and operational difficulties that lead to changes, which in turn lead to extra funding requirements. In the case of national defence, if elected officials choose to spend significantly more money on ships, then there may end up being less funding available for the needs of the army, navy, or air force. Major cost overruns can lead to project failure—the cancellation or delay of procurement. This happens far too often.

But the time had come to replace many capital assets at the DND. After our work on the F-35s, the questions from members of Parliament and media quickly shifted to when we were going to start costing the National Shipbuilding Procurement Strategy.

We started with a blank page, looking at Arctic patrol ships, surface combat ships, joint support ships, offshore science vessels, and icebreakers. That is a tall order. Where do you start with this costing? Would some purchases be more risky than others in the eyes of the treasury? Would some parts of such a procurement be less complex from a costing perspective? If that were true, it would have implications for our team. We could potentially wrap our collective heads around the more simple parts of the purchase in order to build a base of knowledge. That in turn would allow us to take our tool box to the next project within the shipbuilding strategy. After all, we had to walk before we could run, in something of this dimension. It was better to start with a project that would lend itself to learning and future understanding.

This particular request for costing work came jointly from two members of Parliament—Jack Harris, the NDP member for St. John's East and official opposition critic for national defence; and John McKay, the Liberal member for Scarborough–Guildwood. Both were seasoned veterans on procurement issues, whose experience allowed them to quickly establish terms of reference for the project and to understand how we were proposing to carry out the task. It was decided that, with help from Sahir, we would do an independent cost assessment of the joint support ships project, and assess the feasibility of replacing Canada's auxiliary oiler replenishment ships with two JSS ships within the allocated funding envelope of $2.6 billion. The old ships had simply outlived their usefulness. There was no question; they had to be replaced.

Our first challenge was that we knew little about ships. So we assembled an international review panel of experts to help us, including Dr. Daniel Nussbaum from the Naval Postgraduate School, Dr. Norman Friedman from the U.S. Naval Institute, as well as Captain Per Bigum Christensen from the Danish Defence Acquisition and Logistic Organization. We also asked for and received assistance from the Congressional Budget Office and Government Accountability Office in the United States. The relationship we had developed during that first visit we made to the CBO back in 2008 was paying off.

The second challenge was that we lacked sufficient data about the design of the JSS. Given that reality, we were going to have to attempt to cost a replacement for an existing ship. It was not ideal, but it was all we could manage given the circumstances. Think of it as costing a replacement for your current automobile, assuming it is at the end of its useful life. You want to replace that car with something of similar capacity, but the one you intend to purchase hasn't even been built yet—it is still being designed. That was the problem we were facing.

The third challenge was that we would need a model with data that would allow us to build some cost estimates. This is the fun part for financial people. We eventually decided on a cost-estimating tool developed by Price Systems (a Washington, DC, firm) that had applications for both military and nonmilitary purchases. We called on their chief scientist, Arlene Minkiewicz, to serve as an expert reviewer. Then we assigned to the task Tolga Yalkin, the man who had been the principal author on our F-35 estimates, along with a brilliant new analyst from the Treasury Board, Erin Barkel. As with the F-35 project, we felt we had an opportunity to provide analysis to Canadians and parliamentarians that they had never seen before. We used a costing model and a rich database that drew comparisons with similar ships on engineering, manufacturing complexity, and structure. Over time, we were able to come up with a range of estimates and confidence levels on the cost of JSS. Our analysis indicated that the government had not set aside sufficient funds for such a complex procurement. Instead of $2.6 billion for two JSS ships, we suggested that at least $3.2 billion and likely much more would be needed to buy them. We also learned that key personnel within the navy privately agreed with our estimates.

The reaction to this report was far different from the response we had previously received on the F-35. We did not experience any of the intimidation we had witnessed during the F-35 release, either from the government or other sections of the public service. Retired navy experts showed up to our briefings and generally supported the analysis and conclusions. In this environment, the report was used largely to verify the "gut checks" of experts. On the other hand, neither the government nor the public service provided any other type of concrete fiscal analysis. The PBO report received a lot of press coverage because it remained the only show in town. The government would vacate the analytical space to a handful of experts at the budget office.

These two reports—public service compensation and the costing of the new joint support ships—evaluate significant projects consuming tens of billions of taxpayers' dollars. If not for the work of the PBO, our members of Parliament and all Canadians would not have received any information on how these expenditures were going to be managed by the government. If our democratic Parliament had been functioning as intended, you would have received information from your government first and the PBO second. That did not happen. You got information from the PBO only. That should concern you greatly.

THIRTEEN
SEE YOU IN COURT

Throughout my term as PBO, we continually asked various departments of the federal government for fiscal information. Those requests almost always ended with little or no compliance. That happened year after year. We started by asking politely for their data so we could do reasonable costings as part of our mandate. When that didn't work, we tried begging them to release data. As a last resort, we even tried threatening—all to no avail. The country had a brand-new majority Conservative government that had just released its budget for 2012. We needed to examine the departmental and agency spending plans of that budget so parliamentarians might understand the impact of restraints on various public services. But again we had one major problem, and it was always the same problem: no spending plans were made available to us from the government. I've heard that one definition of insanity is doing the same thing over and over while expecting different results each time. It was becoming apparent that, for us, insanity was continuing to expect cooperation from the government in spite of its continual noncooperation. We had to try something different in an attempt to get the needed information—and in the process keep our sanity.

We came up with a novel plan. We would attempt a letter-writing campaign directed specifically at individual deputy ministers. All of those deputy ministers are public servants who get paid a lot of taxpayer money to run departments that deliver programs and services to Canadians. They are also accountability officers, and the government had decided that a good part of their performance pay would be tied to the deputy ministers' ability to deliver on the Budget 2012 fiscal objectives. I thought that if deputies were getting evaluated on their spending plans, it would also be a good idea to allow Canadians and parliamentarians to evaluate the quality of their plans. That, I believe, is fundamental to how our Westminster-model parliamentary system should operate. Members of Parliament needed to know where the restraint was going to bite before they voted on appropriations for departments. That was especially important so that they would have information for their constituents before they returned home to their respective ridings for the summer.

Our letter-writing efforts failed miserably. With the exception of some smaller agencies that reported to Parliament, such as the Auditor General's Office, the deputies from all major spending departments refused to provide their spending plans. We sent three rounds of letters during the spring and summer of 2012 but received virtually nothing for our efforts. That meant that parliamentarians received virtually nothing as well. After each round of letters, the media would report on the lack of cooperation we were experiencing from the public service. It was the civil servants' job as well to ensure that taxpayers knew what was going on in Ottawa. But Ottawa was back in lockdown when it came to the sharing of any meaningful information, whether that data might come from the government directly or from high-level civil servants.

It was fairly obvious to me that this was all being centrally managed by the Privy Council Office. So we wrote another letter, this time to the Clerk of the Privy Council, asking for needed information. At one point in the spring I met with the clerk, Wayne Wouters. He was a former boss of mine at the Treasury Board and the Department of Fisheries and Oceans and I had enjoyed working for him. We had played hockey many years ago and had the occasional beer together. The meeting took place in the clerk's office in the Langevin Block. Wayne indicated that he was sending me a letter saying that he could not share information with us because of rules with the unions that they should be notified in advance. I thought this was a little odd from a parliamentary perspective because it only served to highlight that the austerity measures in Budget 2012 were being implemented without any plans provided to members of Parliament. I told Wayne not to send the letter because we had already been in touch with the unions and they supported our efforts to promote transparency; they also wanted to know what the plans were. But it was too late. Wayne had already sent the letter. Our conversation then shifted to the current environment. Wayne used careful language but clearly insinuated that it was the government's decision not to share its spending plans. I told Wayne, "It is not the prime minister's name on the bottom of the letters saying the PBO (and Parliament by extension) are not going to get the plans; it is your name and you represent the public service." I reminded him that the civil service had a duty to Parliament. Here was another example that the trouble with normal is that it always gets worse: things had sunk to a new low for Parliament and Canadians. Any hopes I had that the new majority government would be more open and transparent were gone in that instant.

What was I to do? The stonewalling was only intensifying. I did not want to be remembered as the parliamentary budget officer who witnessed the last vestiges of any fiscal transparency collapse during his watch. Five years on, I did not want to look back and say to myself (or see it written by someone else) that I had stood by and done nothing for Parliament and Canadian taxpayers at this pivotal moment. Something drastic had to be done. We had exhausted virtually all of our options—except one. So it was at that point that we began looking at legal measures that might allow us to get the data we were seeking. Tolga and Sahir started formulating a legal strategy.

Initially, we considered suing the deputy ministers and government for failing to provide crucial information on government spending. We were well aware that this would be a David versus Goliath battle. If we were going to take on that challenge, we felt that first and foremost we would have to score some kind of win in the court of public opinion. That would include MPs and the media, along with average Canadian citizens. Winning in the court of public opinion meant that we would need to use the PBO website to fire a volley of letters at deputies in the various departments. This allowed members of the media to keep track of the more than sixty departments that were not sharing their spending plans with budget cuts to Parliament. CBC journalist Kady O'Malley frequently tweeted and wrote about it. Winning in the court of public opinion also meant that I would not turn down an opportunity to talk to MPs, experts at conferences, or members of the media on the importance of those spending plans to our democracy and public finance system.

In June 2012 we posted to our website a legal opinion written by University of Ottawa law professor Joseph Magnet, with assistance provided by Tolga. As a first salvo, the two deconstructed the conditions on why the deputy ministers were bound by law (as outlined in the Act of Parliament) to provide spending information to Parliament and the PBO. That launched the ball back into the court of the Clerk of the Privy Council, as MPs and public servants headed off to their summer cottages. It also signalled to the media that we had initiated a legal strategy—this wouldn't be just a one-time thing. The strategizing went on for months as we tried to engage the press as well as the public so as to rally support. Professor Magnet kept telling us that if we were to have any chance of succeeding, that court of public opinion would have to be on our side. If not, he noted that our chances for a win in an actual court of law would be greatly diminished.

Early in the fall of 2012, the Clerk of the Privy Council wrote a letter to me that I subsequently posted to our website. In it was the implication that the PBO mandate did not involve analyzing government operations; in other words, we were overreaching by asking for specific details. This struck me as a blatant attempt to get us to back off. It was misleading, to boot, because although budget plans are required for operations that make up a significant proportion of the nation's finances, the public service tried to downplay the need to provide such plans to Parliament. The clerk suggested that we were already receiving adequate amounts of information, which simply was not correct. Getting any data over time was akin to attempting to pull teeth from the various departments. Yet the clerk stood on the idea that we did not require or have the right to see any plans specific to how the public service was going to freeze discretionary spending over a five-year period.

It was now November 2012 and my term at the PBO was quickly running out, with my exit having been planned for March 2013. It had been a tough go in many respects. As my last few months in the office began, I became somewhat reflective as I thought about both my current position and my entire career as a civil servant. I will confess that it was tempting to simply ride off into the sunset—clean out the office when the time came and get ready for whatever the future might hold away from government life. But as the clock wound down, I felt a real and powerful obligation to my team at the PBO—all of those men and women had been along for this difficult assignment. And I also felt an obligation to the next person who would be sitting at my desk. I determined that I was not going to leave the office with a whimper.

It was now or never if we intended to have a public hearing on a couple of key issues involving the role of the PBO that had dogged us almost from the time our office had been created. All of us in the office felt that we needed to stand up once and for all on these issues—namely, access to information, and the mandate of our office. And so, after seeking opinions from our legal team, I decided to take the government to federal court. I would argue for access to documents and information relating to the previous year's budget. In addition (and again in no small measure for the sake of the next PBO), I also asked that the mandate of the office be clarified. We needed that reference opinion on whether or not it was within our legislative mandate to examine spending restraint. We had tried everything else over time in an effort to secure documents and data. All those efforts had failed. This represented our last gasp.

The PBO was the applicant and the leader of the official opposition, Thomas Mulcair of the NDP, was the respondent. The PBO was in a position where it could not respond to the request for analysis by the leader of the official opposition because information was not forthcoming from the government on departmental spending plans. The public service, Hill bureaucracy, speakers, and government were all thrown into a loop by the legal strategy developed by Tolga. We determined that there should not be a lawsuit. Rather, we decided simply to seek an opinion from the court about our mandate. Canadians from across the country as well as many in the media seemed supportive. The reality is that I really had no other choice given the lack of cooperation from various government departments over data germane to their budgets. In hindsight, perhaps the government wanted this kind of showdown; perhaps they saw in it an opportunity to reshape the PBO. They could claim that it had all been initiated at the request of the person in charge of the office, and they would be correct. The bottom line is that I did what I felt had to be done in such circumstances. Finance Minister Jim Flaherty, Foreign Affairs Minister John Baird, and Treasury Board Secretary Tony Clement all contended at various times that I was exceeding my mandate and position as the PBO. I disagreed with their assertions of my partisan intentions then, and I respectfully continue to disagree with them to this day. My belief was that the court should have its say as to what the PBO mandate should or should not include.

CBC radio host Anna Maria Tremonti once asked me during an interview if we deliberately went after "hot button issues" during my time as the PBO. I told her yes, that is exactly what we did. Why? It was not a strategy designed to embarrass anyone in particular; I can assure you of that. Rather, by addressing some key targets such as our Old Age Security program, I felt that we might inspire Canadians to become more engaged in what their government does and how it conducts its business. If, in the process of such deliberations, the government was found to be loose in its estimates from time to time, whose fault was that? Mine for pointing it out, or the government's for providing poor estimates? You can answer that one however you choose, but at the PBO we felt that transparency was vital on big issues in order to hold people accountable.

The court proceedings that we undertook in the spring of 2013 were greatly ironic in many respects. Those proceedings got underway just as I was preparing to leave the PBO in late March. My last two days on the job as Canada's first parliamentary budget officer were spent in a courtroom attempting to secure a positive reference opinion for our mandate. And of course, the court battle was clearly pointed at the federal government and, inevitably, the person at the head of that government who, as history shows, hired me to the position. Who says Canadian politics is always boring? There is an old saying that "Coincidences are messages from the soul." There we were, in my last two days on the job, in a legal battle fighting over transparency and the importance of accountability in a federal court. The soul of the PBO was intact.

Then, suddenly, time ran out. The clock simply stopped ticking on my term as PBO and just like that, it was over. On my last day, I collected my belongings after returning from the court proceedings, which were ongoing. I left the office that I had occupied in the Sun Life building for the last time and headed back to private life.

I would do many exit interviews in the weeks immediately following the conclusion of my term as PBO. Many of the men and women of the press who had supported us along the journey spent time with me reflecting on my five years on the job. CBC journalist Terry Milewski at one point joked when he asked me, "Is this another *exclusive* exit interview?" I basically did interviews with all the major networks. The circle was complete.

Three months after my term was over, the federal court issued a mixed opinion on the points of order we had argued during those last two days. On the one hand, it was indicated that the Parliamentary Budget Office would need to go back to the government and public service one more time for any needed information. On the other hand, the court would be prepared to rule on the issue of mandate and information acquisition at a future date. The court also indicated that if the government did not want a Parliamentary Budget Office, it should change the act of Parliament. It was a shot across the bow to the government.

I watched from my home as the news broke on television, then took our dog Marley for a walk to celebrate.

FOURTEEN
THE FUTURE OF PUBLIC SERVICE IN CANADA

The public service in Canada needs an overhaul. Normal isn't good enough. Canadians cannot accept the old "just following orders" justification that has permeated many levels of the public service within our country. That's too easy an out. It is often convenient and expedient as public servants to shovel dirt on politicians and institutions so as to deflect attention away from our own vices. But eventually the time comes when you have to look in the mirror and own up. That time is now. We need a debate on what exactly constitutes an effective public service. After all, Canadians are paying big money for the services that are provided—it takes somewhere around $43 billion per year to sustain the public service. Just as our politicians must be held accountable for their roles in leading the country, so must our public servants be held accountable as well. It's only fair and right.

Assessing and reinventing the public service is important and complex, and I bring different experiences, conflicted thoughts, and varying emotions to bear on the topic. If you truly desire change in a meaningful way within any organization, you first need to ask basic questions of "why" and "what" and "how." Why is change within the public service necessary, and how can that change be achieved?

I found myself at different times during my career as a civil servant asking, "What values do we hold as public servants?" If you can accurately answer that question, then it inevitably leads to the next: "Am I true to those values?" I think of my old boss Munir Sheikh, the former chief of Statistics Canada who resigned over the loss of the long-form census, and admire the fact that he obviously knew what he valued, and no paycheque could dissuade him from being true to those values. Unfortunately, that kind of honour is uncommon. Civil servants collectively have struggled to keep true to those values of public service.

There are some fundamental concepts that members of the public service must, as a profession, attend to. For example, what are the ideals that public servants should aspire to? Do public servants even get to have those ideals? Are they prepared to reexamine and reshape ideas associated with public service? These are not easily answered queries. Noam Chomsky, the great political commentator and activist, writes in his book *Necessary Illusion*, "While recognizing that there is rarely anything strictly new under the sun, still we can identify some moments when traditional ideas are reshaped, a new conscious-ness crystallizes and the opportunities that lie ahead appear in new light."

The former clerk of the PCO, my colleague Wayne Wouters, tried to address renewal in a practical manner in his document entitled "Blueprint 2020." For instance, it calls for a bottom-up or grassroots approach to renewal which, to my way of thinking, exacerbates the dilemma of subpar leadership. Sorry, but I have real doubts as to whether the current set of public service leaders in this country are prepared to lead a true renewal exercise in a shortened time frame. If there is to be meaningful renewal from within the public service, it must come from a new generation of public servants. The four guiding principles of Blueprint 2020 do not seem to spark, call for, or inspire any meaningful renewal. The principles are:

- An open and networked environment that engages citizens and partners for the public good;

- A whole-of-government approach that enhances service delivery and value for money;

- A modern workplace that makes smart use of new technologies to improve networking, access to data and customer service; and

- A capable, confident and high-performing workforce that embraces new ways of working and mobilizing the diversity of talent to serve the country's evolving needs.[4]

These are bland and uncontroversial principles. Who can possibly be against a networked environment, better service delivery, modern workplaces, and new ways of working? Unfortunately, none of these four points addresses the obvious elephant in the room, which is that *the public service has stopped showing its work.*

Its capacity to fulfill its duties has been so severely eroded as to make the public service virtually impotent. Its ability to examine issues that will impact future generations of Canadians is in doubt. For instance, how are public servants going to fulfill their responsibilities to Aboriginal peoples in the future? How will they deal with gas emissions and the environment? And how will they deliver health care in a timely and cost-efficient

---

[4] Clerk of the Privy Council, Introduction to Blueprint 2020, accessed May 10, 2015, at http://www.clerk.gc.ca/eng/feature.asp?pageId=350.

way? Civil servants and legislators need to work together to envision imaginative and practical solutions. Only then can we look at how these policies will be funded.

That is fiscal capacity, which is another area to consider. For example, will Canada have the financial capacity to ensure that our national finances are in sound order for the long term? The answer to that question will impact our ability to cost and procure in areas such as the F-35 or ships or future military operations in general. Where is the fiscal sustainability analysis of the public service for the country? How do we know when files are being appropriately costed, if we never see the analysis from public servants? Does it bother the public service that our appropriations system is broken or that omnibus bills have become the norm in order to push legislation through Parliament with limited debate? Do civil servants not see themselves as caretakers of these institutions anymore? What will happen to our service capacity after direct program spending and operational spending is frozen for five years, as is the stated objective of the current government? In real and practical terms, will the freezing of such operation expenditures hinder our ability to pull someone out of the water off the Grand Banks in a rescue effort? Will that policy affect our ability to provide meat in the marketplace that all Canadians will know is safe to consume? Those things take money. We need planning in that regard and numbers to show what government policies will cost—in dollars and cents and, most importantly, in human terms. These aren't economic models; they are real-life applications of the impact policy can have on everyone in the nation in their daily lives. We do not currently possess viable answers for these kinds of questions because the deputy ministers will not show their plans to Parliament. They still refuse *even after the budget officer went to federal court* over the lack of transparency. Is there a rock bottom? Will we need some kind of crisis in order to turn these attitudes around?

George Orwell said that "to see what is in front of one's nose is a constant struggle." I believe that the public service was not ready for a government that emphasized ideology over evidence-based decision making. Previous renewal exercises did not ask the question of how the public service would remain true to its values with a government that focused on ideology. We did not—perhaps, could not—see what was ahead. I hope that the current public service renewal exercise can spark an ethically informed public conversation. I truly believe that many in the rank and file membership are ready for renewal. I suppose that if the leadership in this regard will not come from the top, then it must by necessity originate from the base. Blueprint 2020 is good as far as it goes—a number of inoffensive principles. However, I do not think there is coherence in the public service as it currently exists or looks to exist moving forward.

The context for renewal can begin with the Values and Ethics Code for the Public Sector, which came into effect as of April 2012. Under the code, the *democratic values* of a public servant outline the responsibility to help ministers, under law, to serve the public interest. The code says that public servants shall support both individual and collective ministerial accountability and provide Parliament and Canadians with information on the results of their work. In this respect, we have not lived up to our values in recent times. When Parliament asked the government and public service for information on the F–35 or crime bills or the departmental spending plans consistent with Budget 2012, it was not forthcoming. That is not acceptable.

Additionally, under the code, the *professional values* of a public servant are to serve with competence, excellence, efficiency, objectivity, and impartiality. It says that how ends are achieved in the public service should be as important as the achievements themselves. It also notes that public servants should strive to ensure that the value of transparency in government is upheld while respecting their duties of confidentiality under the law. In this regard, the public service has again fallen short. The public service has allowed the executive branch of government to make omnibus budget bills a standard practice. In doing so, the government and public service have allowed parliamentary debate and scrutiny to suffer. We are complicit in the facilitation of speedy passage of complicated laws. Was the public service not complicit when Parliament found the government in contempt for lack of transparency in 2011? That's not good enough for a profession that aspires to higher ethics and values.

The *ethical values* section of the code speaks to a public service reflecting the need to act at all times in such a way as to uphold the public trust. It says that public servants shall act at all times in a manner that will bear the closest public scrutiny, an obligation that is not fully discharged by simply acting within the law. This does not happen when deputy ministers refuse to provide spending plans to Parliament and the PBO that outline where Budget 2012 cuts will take place, along with an explanation of how those cuts will affect services to the public. Shame on all of us for sticking our collective heads in the sand.

Finally, under the code, the *people values* stipulate that public servants should demonstrate respect, fairness, and courtesy in their dealings with both citizens and fellow public servants. It says that appointment decisions in the public service shall be based on merit and that public service values should play a key role in recruitment, evaluation, and promotion. This did not happen with the recruitment of the new PBO.

What I learned from my PBO experience is that our public service has become good at avoiding accountability and transparency. The result is that public trust in the public service declines. Jane Jacobs, the famous American-Canadian urban activist, said "the absence of trust is inimical to a well-run society." If only we could institutionalize trust, but alas, that is impossible. Our public service leaders are going to have to step up and *earn* trust! To my friends and colleagues in the public service, I say this: Blueprint 2020, more than anything else it espouses, must be about restoring trust to the public service in Canada.

I believe that, as a nation, all of us have increasingly become prisoners to a kind of politics of fear. This is an old and effective political weapon, one which the current government has no doubt used to its advantage. Careers are at stake. If you speak up and disagree, you could be punished or even dismissed. Yet, the disposition to disagree is the lifeblood of an open society. I sense that the federal public service was not ready to handle the likes of a government that had a strong ideology and not a strong disposition to analysis or evidence. I believe that public servants must share accountability with elected representatives as the caretakers of institutions. Perhaps we have taken for granted the institutions, programs, services, and rights that we have inherited. The power of the purse in our Westminster system of parliamentary government rests with the House of Commons, not the executive. We have behaved otherwise. We have acquiesced and risked accepting the current situation as normal, but as it exists, this situation isn't normal. It's what we as citizens have allowed to be perceived as normal, that's all. We have accommodated the general erosion of our democratic processes and institutions to occur over time. We need to change that normal.

The stakes are high. Our institutions have been degraded. The majority of Canadian citizens along with the civil service have become disillusioned and indifferent. The research on the importance of strong institutions is growing and the discussion getting louder. I absolutely believe that public service renewal is part of democratic renewal. As we think about public service renewal, let us not be fearful of asking the basic questions that speak to our core purpose as public servants. Let us not be fearful about being honest about whether we are living up to our values.

In 2013, five previous Clerks of the Privy Council were honoured at a public policy forum in Toronto. While I had worked for all of them in some capacity, I had worked just down the hall from three of them. Their advice as leaders of the public service was almost always cogent, timely, and important.

Alex Himelfarb noted that organizational models of authority and information sharing are transforming. To reinvent itself in response to these changes, he says, the public service must become more creative, open, and connected to Canadians. Mel Cappe noted that although public servants should not talk publicly about "policy," they "should be encouraged to talk to the public about their science and their research." Cappe indicated that "some ministers" were preventing public servants from doing this now. I agree with Mel and am fervent in my conviction that public servants need to do their work, show their work, and stand up for their work. But in order to do that, the public service leaders of the future must set a high bar for transparency. Without transparency, ideas will not be generated and shared. There will be no accountability for the executive or public service. There will be only fear.

In all of these spheres, a strong public service can act to help form policies that advance the country. The choice is ours—renewal or more of the same.

FIFTEEN
THE SURVIVAL OF THE PBO

I was once labelled as a bald, kind of nerdy looking guy with glasses (thanks, Steve Paikin) and I really can't argue with that description. Eventually, the minister of finance said that I was "unbelievable, unreliable, and incredible." But over time, and given the very believable, reliable, and credible work done by a dedicated group of individuals at the PBO, my team and I were proven more than capable in the mission we undertook. In spite of the many distractions created by various agencies of the government, our work stood up to scrutiny. All the rhetoric and diversionary attempts simply meant that the government wanted to steer people away from the substance of an issue through innuendo, insinuation, and good old-fashioned name-calling.

The prime minister made an interim appointment after my time was up as parliamentary budget officer. Suffice it to say that the appointee lacked the kind of budgeting experience that should be a prerequisite for the PBO. Very qualified professionals were available for the post, and many of them could easily have been found within that group of "public service refugees" who already occupied positions within the office. To add injury to insult, a couple of extremely qualified candidates—two deputy officers at the PBO—were bypassed for interviews beyond the second round. Both were senior civil servants who understand the portfolio, yet both received only a cursory look. Whatever the reason for this, the loss is real.

The PM is accountable for his actions, the actions of his office, and the quality of his appointments, whether they are to the Senate or the PBO. Jean-Denis Fréchette, who was eventually appointed to the position on a permanent basis, has no meaningful budgeting experience. Further, the weak legislation that underpins the PBO will not sustain the office, let alone allow for growth and development. If we cherish transparency, if we value independent analytic expertise, then we need to strengthen the office. If the PBO is allowed to be unwound by the government, the type of quality fiscal analysis we provided will be lost to parliamentarians who are not a part of the executive. All indications are that it will be unwound in some form or another. Once my term was about to end, I gave indications that I was in no big hurry to leave. I offered to stay on as PBO when my term ended until a successor could be named after a fair and open process. Yet the very process for securing my replacement as the next parliamentary budget officer was compromised by the presence on the panel of a Conservative staffer who was chief of staff for Government House Leader Peter Van Loan. A senior Privy Council Office official was on the hiring panel as well. In short, this first attempt by the government to "transparently" appoint a new PBO was anything but an independent process. It reeked of secrecy and partisanship right from the start. There was no public announcement of who was on the interview panel.

What can a government gain from an independent PBO? My standard response to that question in recent years has always been "probably not very much." But my comrade in arms at the PBO, Mostafa Askari, takes exception to that response, and believes that the government has a tremendous amount to gain from a vibrant and accountable PBO. He maintains that the office can serve to strengthen the government's hand when it comes to the efficient operation of financial matters. I have come around to Mostafa's way of thinking, now that I am out of the position. But that avoidance of accountability is in reality a great loss for the country—for our democracy. All of the secrecy and lack of transparency that Prime Minister Harper had so adamantly railed against when he was in opposition remains in effect to this day. But he was correct to call for the creation of such an office. Unfortunately, once he gained power, things changed and he started to backpedal. A new government needs to reconstitute the PBO. I have been outspoken on the need to strengthen the legislation that created the PBO in order to strengthen the PBO itself. Opposition parties supported a private member's bill to that effect in 2012, while government members did not. Those are the facts. Without that strengthening of the legislation and the mandate, we will lose something. If we don't demand it, we will lose something. How can we let such a vital part of our democracy unravel or become dormant?

During and after my time in the office, I received both positive support and negative criticism from many sources about how I conducted myself. In some cases, those comments were about my office's relationship to the media. I was criticized by some for being too present in the front pages of newspapers. Other times, I read opinions questioning the methodologies we used to procure data. Both praise and criticism were probably justifiable to some degree and evidence of a healthy democracy. As just one example, once my time was up as PBO and shortly after I accepted the position of Jean-Luc Pépin Research Chair on Canadian Government at the University of Ottawa, I read a scathing op-ed from Philip Cross, a former senior economist at Statistics Canada, in which he questioned some of my tactics while at the helm of the PBO. The details of that criticism aren't important. What *is* important is that Philip got the chance to register it in the popular press. Did I agree with it? No. But should he be vilified for expressing those opinions? Absolutely not. Rather, we need that kind of transparent exchange.

This book has been an attempt to represent òne public servant's perspective on government operations and the civil service in our country. I've described events I experienced as head of the PBO to illustrate why it is so difficult to make positive change in a bureaucracy such as the civil service. It's difficult, but it is essential nevertheless. Those of us who were involved in that "beautiful experiment," as Sahir so eloquently called his time at the PBO, believe that real change *is doable*. Too often the collective reaction to meaningful change is, "This is the way we have always done it." For some reason, that rationale seems to retain its traction across generations of politicians and public servants. There might be lip service and political rhetoric offered at appropriate moments, but in reality things are only getting worse on the ground. Sadly, it continues to be business as usual. "Normal" is winning the day. Major revision and rebirth needs to occur in the public service if Canadians are going to get their money's worth moving forward.

There is a lot at stake here. We need independent fiscal institutions such as the PBO to help our political leaders do their jobs more effectively. The old axiom "information is power" is real, and the power needs to be with all of our elected officials, not just the executive branch. While trepidation or even fear continues to grip many of the people who serve as MPs, some have become vocal in their support of the PBO. I applaud each and every one of them. For example, NDP deputy finance critic Guy Caron was quoted as saying that our plans were "good news for accountability" while also criticizing the appointment process for the next PBO. Caron has also noted that "It's very obvious that when the Conservatives created this office, it was all smoke and mirrors. For such an office to work well, it needs to be fully independent." I couldn't agree more.

Even in times of majority governments, no one in power can ever be one hundred percent immune to controversy. Sometimes it begins within the ranks. Increasingly, we are seeing cracks in the Conservative mortar, perhaps best evidenced by independent Alberta MP Brent Rathgeber who left the Conservative caucus, noting that Parliament's ability to hold government to account for its spending is worsening, a central tenet of this book. He stated, for the record, "We have this huge, huge void where the government is introducing budgets, but they're not being subject to adequate and in some cases any scrutiny. The government really goes out of its way to clip Parliament's wings when it does try to scrutinize what it does. I think it's critical that other institutions step up where Parliament is unable to."[5]

Those two men have spoken to the very essence of what the PBO needs to look like if we want meaningful change in the way our government conducts the business of its people.

So, what of the future? Where is Canada being taken by our leadership? How will the PBO stand up over time? As noted previously, no economist is in possession of a crystal ball and no one can forecast the future with absolute certainty. But part of what an economist must do is try to gauge what *could* happen in our future through projections based on the best current available data. Three major challenges face our country when it comes

---

[5] Michael Woods, "Former parliamentary budget officer Kevin Page's new plans greeted as a victory for accountability," Canada.com, July 29, 2013, accessed May 10, 2015, at http://o.canada.com/news/national/former-parliamentary-budget-officer-kevin-pages-new-plans-greeted-as-a-victory-for-accountability.

to our ability to manage our finances. Whoever wins the 2015 national election will confront political challenges, economic challenges including fiscal policy, and finally, challenges related to renewal of the public service and Parliament.

On the political front, polling numbers have shifted considerably since the last federal election. This has been driven in part by leadership changes to the opposition parties along with the challenges of governing that the Conservative Party has experienced. A case could be made that the numbers are tightening. Current projections suggest that a majority government is not in the cards in 2015. Let's hope that the polling numbers— which we know politicians watch (whether those numbers are correct or not)—help to create more positive pressure so as to raise the level and clarity of debate during the election campaign.

A useful question must be, "Who will occupy the high road?" Right now, that path would appear to be somewhat vacant. For example, when it comes to issues such as the Senate spending scandal, what we are actually dealing with is the very human need for basic trust. That issue of trust is the preeminent and most necessary of ingredients for whoever looks to lead. And certainly, once trust has been lost by any politician or leader, it cannot easily be won back. Unfortunately, we cannot institutionalize trust—it has to be earned by our leaders, day after day. The American writer Upton Sinclair said a hundred years ago that "it is difficult to get a man to understand something when his salary depends on his not understanding it." This issue of trust should be at the top of the various election platforms. The Senate spending issue is a distraction. It has real potential to drag on for many reasons and to the detriment of the government, which will end up bearing much of the blame. Ironically, the entire situation could create positive pressure to shift focus to a priorities and policy agenda. Whether the Senate should be elected or not, or exist at all, should be an election issue. Yes, we most certainly need sober second thought. Yes, we need regional perspectives. Yes, we need checks and balances on power. And yes, we desperately need strong institutions. Whether the Senate will be a part of the solution—or simply remain a part of the problem—is anybody's guess. Forecasting costs is a lot simpler than trying to predict the future of the Canadian Senate!

Albert Einstein once noted that "in the middle of difficulty you will find opportunity." The challenge for Canada's current political parties and leadership is to take this opportunity and shift the current political dysfunction to function. Ottawa is a mess and, unfortunately, the sad truth is that many of its politicians are not trusted. That needs to be fixed.

Economic, Fiscal, and Policy Context and Challenges

A real challenge for the next federal leaders will be how short-term economic uncertainty can hinder effective long-term planning. The challenge is fiscal choice. In the current context, should the federal government stay the course toward medium-term fiscal balance, or do they move forward with some bold initiatives to address longer-term challenges? There is a need to strengthen potential output growth, and to address social challenges related to aging demographics and rising inequality and environmental sustainability. But can any government in the short term muster the courage to tackle such core issues as the long-term good of the country? An aging population and the resultant need for more beds in full caring nursing homes is not a sexy topic for the populace. It will take courage for leaders to deliver relevant policy changes for those types of issues. And it will take some extraordinary spin makers to help sell it all.

From a purely economic perspective, the short- and medium-term planning outlook for the Speech from the Throne will not likely change significantly from Budget 2014. Modest growth in 2014 and into 2015 will eventually lead to the output gap closing in 2016. There remains relatively high international uncertainty with notable downside risks. The federal government has not received the positive upward surprises that helped governments during the first decade of this century. We have seemingly gone from crisis to crisis since the 2008 crash. From the banking crisis to fiscal solvency/sustainability issues in the European Union and the United States to rising concerns in emerging econo-mies, the list goes on. It has been a complicated time in world economic history. Uncertainty, relatively weak international outlook, Canadian fiscal restraint, and household de-leveraging will keep a lid on domestic growth and keep our unemployment rate stubbornly higher than our political leaders would like.

The current federal government has made a conscious polit-ical choice to balance the budget over the next few years. We are in a period of austerity while our economy operates below potential. The current deficit is partly cyclical and partly struc-tural. If the federal government achieves its spending restraint objectives, we will be in a structural surplus position over the medium term. Discretionary spending relative to gross domestic product (GDP) will be at historic lows. There will be fiscal room to manoeuvre. There is fiscal choice. Reducing the rate of growth of the Canada Health Transfer (CHT) and freezing direct program spending for five years suggests the federal government has a sustainable fiscal framework over the long term (in terms of stabilizing debt to GDP). This is an enviable position for the federal government.

There will be a thorough and honest critique of the govern-ment's legacy by media and voters in the lead-up to the 2015 election. In all likelihood, the federal government will have a positive fiscal gap—a position to reduce debt relative to the size of the economy notwithstanding aging demographics. This is also an enviable position. Again, there will be fiscal room to manoeuvre. There will be fiscal choice for whichever party holds power after the election in 2015.

But the reality is that while the federal books will be balanced or in a small surplus by 2016, here is what Canada will look like:

- our long-term debt will be higher;

- economic growth will be weaker (slower productivity growth, with lower employment and participation rates);

- provincial and territorial governments will find themselves faced with increasing costs to administer and deliver health care because the federal government has drastically cut the amount of money it transfers to them for health care spending;

- fiscal sustainability at the provincial and territorial government levels will be a major challenge due to reductions in the Canada Health Transfer escalator;

- there will be an offloading on the crime agenda;

- there will be fiscal and service level risks due to austerity cuts without a transparent plan, a lack of trust in institutions due to omnibus bills, and a lack of decision support analysis on major decisions (for example, Old Age Security, F-35 procurement, spending cuts).

Further, we will be lagging behind in tackling long-term issues regarding productivity growth, aging demographics, income inequality, health care, and the environment.

We will need critical thinking in order to move forward in a positive way on long-term national issues. Cuts to the GST and corporate income taxes and the deficit-financed stimulus package (the Conservative legacy) may seem small in relation to the future efforts required to tackle long-term issues such as the environment (putting a price on carbon, tax reform, green infrastructure, etc.). We have collectively kicked the proverbial can down the road. The hand-off to the next generation is not great and we are leaving them with institutions that are weaker than when we received them.

Finally, health care is a provincial jurisdiction but it is a national issue. The problem is not going to go away without debate, leadership, and change. The future of health care is a real spending issue, not just for the current generation but for future generations as well. It is very fiscally material, unlike the Senate spending issue. It is also complicated and fraught with political risks.

Notwithstanding international uncertainty and relatively slow growth, Canada's fiscal position going into 2015—an election year—is relatively positive. The strategic political challenge for our policy makers is to decide whether we elevate the policy debate now on our longer-term issues, or wait. I think it is in the interests of Canadians—particularly our younger generation—to start the debate on priorities and policy directions immediately. Anything less is tantamount to cowardice from our leaders.

Institutional Context and Challenges

Many of our important national institutions face the challenge of restoring functionality and trust. The bigger challenge is raising understanding that institutions matter, and this is thwarted by indifference and willful blindness. Allen Scheck from the University of Maryland says budgets and budget making are about three things—fiscal discipline, allocating efficiency, and operational efficiency. We spend a lot of time on the first item and do a poor job on the other two. Our Constitution and Financial Administration Act say that the power of the purse rests with the House of Commons. Do we want members of Parliament and senators to have useful information (evidence based) before they vote on appropriations and changes in tax law? I would hope so—yet that is currently not the case in Ottawa.

In the short run, democracies can survive the indifference of the citizens, the so called "democratic deficit," which manifests itself in such areas as the steadily declining turnout at federal and provincial elections, and the cynical distaste for politicians and political institutions. But in the long run, democracies exist only by virtue of the engagement of their citizens in the management of public affairs. We need to be concerned about the democratic deficit. Speaking as a former parliamentary budget officer, I believe we need to fix the system under which our MPs and senators scrutinize spending, as the current system is untenable. Many MPs with whom I have had discussions over the past ten years do not feel inspired to do their jobs because they are not permitted to make changes. The playing field between the executive and the legislature is not level—we have a massive information asymmetry problem. A full review of the process to ensure MPs have incentives to make meaningful change is needed, and it should be as independent an assessment as possible. It is one of those areas where a healthy and arm's length PBO could do an effective job for the country and the men and women who serve it on Parliament Hill. We need to establish financial control gates around program activities that MPs can understand, not the current voting based on inputs such as operations and capital. In addition to a strong legislative budget office, we need public servants to proactively release their evidence-based analysis on policy and costing, as we currently see in the system utilized in New Zealand.

The PBO was an experiment in transparency, showing what could happen if we had a legislative budget office that could counteract unsubstantiated claims made by the government of the day. We had unsubstantiated claims related to the fiscal costs of crime bills and fighter planes, and the PBO was there to supply Parliament with authoritative estimates. In addition, opposition parties can question estimates from the executive and public service, which raises the bar on transparency and can stimulate policy discussion (e.g., on crime bills or fighter planes). This adds complexity, multiple data points, and competition of analysis. Those are all good things for Canadians.

The PBO as it exists at the time of this writing is in danger because the current culture and legislation in Ottawa will not sustain it. As stated throughout this book, we desperately need to create a culture of analysis and transparency within our public service at all levels, a culture that will support and protect analytical dissonance. From a practical perspective, we must renew the legislation that underpins the PBO so as to renew the appointment procedure. This will ensure that all parties as well as the legislature have a say as to who the next PBO will be. Our budget officers should be appointed based on their knowledge and experience, whereas the current PBO is appointed effectively by the PM and works at his pleasure. In such a circumstance my fear is that the current budget officer may not realize that he has blinders on. A recent television show featuring the great Canadian comic Rick Mercer was taped at the Ottawa Winterlude and at the Lions Foundation of Canada Dog Guides headquarters in Oakville. When Mercer was about to take his first solo walk with a guide dog, he was asked to put on blinders. When he said, "This is standard equipment for the new parliamentary budget officer," he got a good laugh, but the comment hit awfully close to home—and it was pretty well on the mark.

The current PBO has never worked on a budget or in a central agency. Would we hire an auditor general who had never worked on an audit? Or would we even contemplate hiring a governor for our central bank who has never worked in a central bank? The answers are obviously no in both cases, yet we have done exactly that in hiring the PBO. There has been a proliferation of legislative budget offices around the world over the past decade, with vastly different mandates (economic/fiscal versus financial) but some common underlying principles and values (transparency). The OECD and IMF have been very supportive of these measures in order to strengthen institutions while developing more fiscal transparency and accountability. There is no "one size fits all," and that should never be allowed to happen. Rather, the specific institutional cultures vary and, in the case of Canada, we need to produce the budget office that we want and need. Recently I was afforded the opportunity to spend a day with Ludovit Odor, who heads up the legislative budget office in the Slovak Republic. The man has a PhD in mathematics/economics as his foundation for the job, and has previously worked at both the ministry of finance and central bank in Slovakia. During his time in public service, he has briefed his prime minister on all kinds of issues related to economic and budget concerns. He is viewed as someone who can give great assistance to the government and is expected to do so in an unbiased and apolitical manner. In a very short time he has managed to build an effective team that has released many important papers, and this remains the vision we must all share when it comes to our own PBO. But that is not the kind of example we currently see happening at home. Unfortunately, the PBO, just like many other of our institutions in Canada, is being increasingly moved toward the deep backwaters. In addition, Prime Minister Harper is also responsible and accountable for the flagrant use of omnibus legislation to limit debate in the House, which undermines accountability and democracy. It is my belief that eventually the prime minister will be held accountable in this regard—it is just a matter of when. But in the meantime, our country will pay a price for these tactics.

It is my hope that the next PBO will be appointed by the legislature and subject to dismissal for cause by said legislature. We need to make the PBO an officer of Parliament, not an officer of the Library of Parliament, and the office must be understood to be totally independent from political and bureaucratic interference if it is to survive and flourish. At present, the officer is responsible to Parliament for the legislative mandate but administratively responsible to the Library of Parliament. Legislative and administrative responsibilities and accountabilities should coincide. No, they *must* coincide.

We need to demand that the principle of transparency be enshrined in legislation associated with the PBO. We need to ensure that both the mandate and budget of the office are consistent such that the people who comprise the PBO can execute their duties. The idea that a fiscal rope can be used to tie the hands of the office is appalling, undemocratic, and downright dangerous. In the end, the democratic deficit in Canada is growing while the fiscal deficit is decreasing. Institutions have been degraded and a majority of Canadians have seemingly become disillusioned. Cynicism is increasing. Indifference is increasing. We are ill advised to ignore these sentiments.

Finally, I have been asked by many colleagues and friends since leaving the PBO position about my own plans for future employment. I still have lots of gas in my professional tank, though most certainly my bridges as a civil servant have all been burned. As of this writing I have accepted a three-year position at the University of Ottawa and am the Jean-Luc Pépin Research Chair on Canadian Government of the Faculty of Social Sciences. Allan Rock, a former MP, justice and health minister, and now the University of Ottawa president and vice-chancellor, feels that this new position is a perfect match, and so do I. He has stated that my "experience in the federal public service will be a major asset in developing the public finance and governance projects we have planned." I hope so! I am deeply honoured to have been chosen for this position and look forward to the next few years with great anticipation. This is an especially meaningful appointment in my eyes given what the chair has as its mandate. This endowed research chair is named in honour of Jean-Luc Pépin, a respected politician and political scientist who was a professor at the University of Ottawa, and is dedicated to research on Canadian political institutions and their transformation in response to the changing conditions and practices of contemporary democratic governance. Over the next few years, it is my intention to go about the business of getting funding for the creation of a new institute dedicated to public finance issues. It will, in many ways, be fashioned after the United Kingdom's Institute of Fiscal Studies, meaning that it will speak with an independent voice and provide timely cost analysis on a variety of issues. It will be a de facto "think tank" with a blended approach to projects with both public sector financial analysis and private contract work as a means to help fund the venture. We will use students in all the projects. And yes, we will be releasing reports on various aspects of federal government spending and taxation.

In addition, I will be afforded the opportunity to teach some courses within the Faculty of Social Sciences: one specific to economics and the other in public administration. This is very exciting for me because I truly believe it is imperative that we nurture the next generation of leaders, and what better place to do that than through a university setting. My early impressions are that our students are not impressed with my generation and the leaders it has put to the top of the class in this country. Many have commented to me that they feel we have not addressed long-term issues. They feel that we have undermined many of the Canadian institutions—*their* institutions—and I tend to agree with the students in this regard.

I look forward to the exchanges I will continue to have with students and faculty colleagues. I feel reinvigorated—very similar to my mood when I began my term as the PBO. I know that if things unfold as I hope, we will have the opportunity to make a positive impact on the lives of all Canadians.

I'm not done yet.

EPILOGUE

My time as Canada's first parliamentary budget officer was my last position as a civil servant for the federal government. But my feeling about the importance of the office has never wavered. Educational philosopher Robert Hutchins once wrote that "The death of democracy is not likely to be an assassination from ambush. It will be a slow extinction from apathy, indifference, and undernourishment." Those words resonate with me as I observe events from a position outside of government for the first time in over thirty years. The indifference is hauntingly observable in Canada, the apathy palpable. There is a growing democratic deficit, an erosion of trust in our institutions. Without some genuine anger and passion for renewal, I don't know where the future might lead. Unfortunately, if any renewal is to take place within the public service, I sense it must come from a new generation of civil servants. My generation has failed miserably in that regard.

There will undoubtedly be plenty of politicians and civil servants who will be queried about some of the information that appears in this book. Perhaps they will be asked to comment on its accuracy. My guess is that many will hedge, do the old "bob and weave," and even lie if they feel they must in order to survive in their jobs. They will accuse me of some kind of political motivation for these writings. Or at worst, they will try to throw someone else under the bus in order to save their own skin. That our elected officials will not accept responsibility for their actions should trouble Canadians. That MPs and high-ranking civil servants behave this way should be unsettling for the entire country. But if my guess is right, most of us will probably take note, sit back, and think, "There's nothing I can do."

And that would be a shame.

We have to uphold the values that underpin our democratic institutions. *We* have to be the ones who stand up to our elected officials and make demands for our country and for our democracy. At what point do we collectively say, "Enough"? Our federal institutions are under attack at a time when secrecy by governments appears to be the increasingly acceptable norm. I witnessed that reality during my time as a member of the public service. But it wasn't always this bad. In times past, there was a public service motto of "fearless advice and loyal implementation" and that credo had been followed by many great deputy ministers of finance, such as David Dodge, Fred Gorbet, and Scott Clark. However, in modern times, the inside joke among public servants is that the motto has now become "loyal advice and fearless implementation." It is difficult to admit, but those of us who have served have too often allowed ourselves to be intimidated to the point where we have failed the public that we serve.

Today I fear that governments and many of the public servants who help run those governments do not want to be held accountable. Politicians might say they do when they are a member of an opposition party or campaigning in an election. Public servants might talk a good game when they get together with colleagues and peers to discuss their performance. But the hard truth is that in most instances neither of these groups seeks accountability; they desire power and responsibility without significant accountability. There isn't a single villain but rather a collective malaise among politicians and senior civil servants. They want to control information in order to keep or acquire power in their departmental fiefdoms. And they surely do not want any resistance.

Governments do not want real debate with elected representatives. Real debate, which would involve informed analysis and exploring options, could be construed as being unsupportive of the political leadership. In today's political environment, that is a no-no. We need to restore the checks and balances in our system of Westminster parliamentary government democracy. *Most importantly, we need to restore the power of the purse to the House of Commons.* Given those needs, we also require a public service that provides fearless advice and loyal implementation in order to maintain the integrity of our public institutions. Is that too much to expect? It shouldn't be.

A healthy and high functioning Parliamentary Budget Office can greatly assist all Canadians in this regard. It was my great honour to serve as PBO those first five years of its existence. Given my son's death, the timing of the job may actually have saved me. The battles, the name-calling, and the innuendo all served to occupy me at a time when I desperately needed to be occupied. So I am grateful to Prime Minister Harper for that appointment. I am grateful to Canadians who embraced our efforts at the PBO. And most importantly, I am especially grateful to my wonderful staff that set a high bar for every public service employee in the country through their efforts at the PBO.

CHRONOLOGY OF MAJOR EVENTS AT THE PARLIAMENTARY BUDGET OFFICE

2008

Canada's first parliamentary budget officer is appointed.

MP Paul Dewar asks PBO to cost Canada's engagement in Afghanistan.

PBO releases costing of Canada's engagement in Afghanistan during middle of election campaign.

PBO receives letter from speakers criticizing the budget office's open and transparent business model.

PBO releases first economic and fiscal outlook calling for recession and deficit.

PBO receives letter from parliamentary librarian indicating the office's budget will be reduced by one third from planned 2008–09 levels.

2009

PBO gets involved in Budget 2009 assessment of fiscal stimulus.

PBO releases major report released on Aboriginal educational infrastructure highlighting underfunding by government.

Joint committee of Library of Parliament meets to discuss operations, independence, and budget of PBO. Former parliamentarians indicate budget officer should be held in contempt of Parliament. Committee wants PBO to release reports only if requesting MPs agree (transparency?).

PBO releases report on economy highlighting worsening economic – and fiscal situation.

PBO releases reports looking at gaps in quarterly reporting on budget and delays in the rollout of infrastructure stimulus.

PBO releases first major report on long-term fiscal sustainability for federal government. Report indicates longer-term fiscal gap due to aging demographics.

2010

Expanded PBO tool box helps MPs better understand depth of recession in an international context and fiscal challenges. Analysis indicates budgetary deficit is part structural and part cyclical. Loss of output projected to be similar to protracted recession in 1990s.

PBO releases report on Employment Insurance program highlighting issues with the government's new independent insurance board as a result of the 2009 economic downturn.

PBO releases report providing a fiscal impact analysis on the Truth in Sentencing Act. The government initially refused to provide parliamentarians with cost estimates. Incarceration is costly to the treasury.

PBO releases report examining differing estimates of economic potential output. The report highlights that the Canadian economy is operating well below its productive potential. Finance department will not release its estimates.

PBO releases major report on eve of G8 and G20 summits on security costing effectively supporting government contention that security costing for summit is a very expensive endeavour.

PBO releases a report on the Infrastructure Stimulus Program. The report, prepared largely by a University of Ottawa student, indicates correctly that the government must expand deadlines for the program. The government changes its deadline.

Updated fall outlook incorporates analysis of uncertainty to better highlight risk around the forecasts and probability analysis of the government achieving its targets.

PBO releases report indicating that PBO and IMF outlook numbers are similar for Canada despite different suggestions from the finance minister.

The Integrated Monitoring Database is introduced, which allows parliamentarians to track spending each quarter with authorities approved. It receives strong support across party lines and from the media and was built for about $30 000 with the help of a very supportive contractor and a student from Carleton University.

2011

PBO releases what could be its most controversial report on the projected costs of the F-35. It suggests life cycle costs will be nearly two times higher than initial government estimates. The report is attacked by the government and public service but later supported by the auditor general and a consulting firm (KPMG) hired by the government.

PBO releases reports on outlook and tax expenditures. The report on tax expenditures highlights a major gap in the parliamentary review process.

PBO releases second major fiscal sustainability report showing a long-term fiscal gap at both the federal and provincial levels of government.

PBO releases analysis indicating that while the government is officially saying there is no structural problem with respect to the federal deficit, finance numbers suggest there is a structural issue.

PBO releases report indicating that the government's change to the Canada Health Transfer will have a major long-term fiscal impact. Analysis indicates the federal fiscal structure is now sustainable but the problem at the provincial level got much bigger.

Minister of finance calls parliamentary budget officer "unbelievable, incredible, and unreliable," yet provides no financial analysis to counter PBO assessment.

PBO releases major report on the cost of the government's tough on crime agenda with respect to tightening restrictions on conditional sentencing.

PBO appears in front of Standing Committee on Government Operations and Estimates on the need to reform the appropriations process. Reforms required to change process, structure of estimates, and support. Question raised whether MPs want the "power of purse" returned to the House of Commons.

2012

Prime minister indicates in Davos, Switzerland, that Old Age Security program is not sustainable and proposes to raise age limit from sixty-five to sixty-seven. PBO releases a report saying OAS is sustainable (supported by chief actuary's assumptions and analysis). The government criticizes but does not release any analysis.

PBO report on economic outlook breaks from private sector and calls for greater short-term economic weakness. The report highlights continued weakness in the United States and negative impact on Canadian economic growth from federal budget reductions announced in Budget 2012.

Attorney general releases bombshell report on F–35 indicating the government had numbers for F–35 life cycle costs.

PBO appears at a tense public accounts committee meeting overseeing the F–35 purchase. In post committee scrum, budget officer replies to CBC reporter Julie Van Dusen that the government was trying to mislead Canadians.

PBO exchanges letters with deputy ministers (three rounds) and Clerk of Privy Council (two rounds) on an information request to get spending plans from departments and agencies consistent with budget objectives calling for major spending restraint.

PBO sends Clerk of Privy Council a legal opinion on why request for budget plan information is within mandate.

PBO develops and implements an online database using nondisclosed program spending information to track spending (restraint) on a program activity basis as it is being implemented.

PBO releases a major long-term fiscal sustainability report that shows the federal government and CPP/QPP are fiscally sustainable but provincial governments are not.

PBO announces that it will seek federal court guidance.

2013

PBO releases a major report on public sector compensation showing that growth in the federal wage envelope is not sustainable.

PBO releases a major report on the costing of joint support ships. The report suggests the government has not set aside sufficient resources.

PBO provides the first-ever cost framework to understand the overall fiscal cost of the Canadian criminal justice system.

On the last two days of the first parliamentary budget officer mandate, the PBO is in federal court on the reference opinion.

ACKNOWLEDGMENTS

The late economist John Maynard Keynes argued that the future is inherently unknowable. Ten years ago, I would not have predicted that I would write a book about the failings of Parliament and what they mean for the future of our country. I would not have predicted that I would be Canada's first parliamentary budget officer.

As my term as Canada's parliamentary budget officer was winding up in March 2013, I found myself at a Churchill Debate at the University of Toronto's Hart House (Resolution: "This House believes that Parliament has been thrown under the Omnibus"). A very distinguished professor of political science, Peter Russell, was there, and said I needed to write down the story of the Parliamentary Budget Office. He said it was an important story that needs to be told. Shortly after, I found myself on a morning CBC radio program hosted by Kathleen Petty. A listener called in and asked when the book was going to come out. When I discussed with my family the possibility of writing the book, it was my Aunt Barb (Couture), the sister of my late father, who gave me the order—write the book.

I decided that if I were going to write a book, it had to be a personal view of what it was like to set up a new institution for

Parliament that was designed to support increased transparency and accountability in an environment that had a history and political and bureaucratic culture of doing everything it could to *evade* transparency and accountability. I wanted a book that would be available to a wider audience, as Parliament is too disconnected from Canadians. There may be opportunities down the road to work on projects of a more technical nature to restore the power of the purse to the House of Commons, but this book would be accessible to all.

I wanted to write a story of what it was like to go from being an obscure back-room public servant to a person in front of parliamentary committees and the media on the major economic and fiscal issues of the day because the government refused to provide the information required to Parliament so it could do its job.

I turned to a friend and retired associate professor at the University of Windsor, Vern Stenlund, to help me write this story. Vern and I grew up in the same city—Thunder Bay. We share the same roots and perhaps, as a result, a way of looking at the world. He had just finished *Bobby Orr: My Story*, a very successful project with the hockey icon Bobby Orr and the Penguin Random House Canada publishing company. Vern is no stranger to the hockey world, and my guess is that there are not too many hockey players drafted in the second round of the NHL that go on to complete a doctorate like he did. Vern also has a passion for writing, and I needed help telling a story to a wide audience. We spent countless hours together talking and writing about the budget officer experience. There were more than a few chuckles. Vern interviewed a number of people—members of the budget office, public servants, political leaders and media—to help make sure we were reflecting a story that was seen and shared by many. It was an honour to work with Dr. Stenlund. He is a true professional.

I want to thank our editor, Diane Turbide of Penguin Random House Canada. As you will read in this book, I am very partial to working with people who love what they are doing and have developed great knowledge from experience. I thank Diane Turbide for her excellent work on this book.

INDEX